50 UNDERWEAR QUESTIONS

A BARE-ALL HISTORY

LLOYD KYI

ILLUSTRATED BY
ROSS KINNAIRD

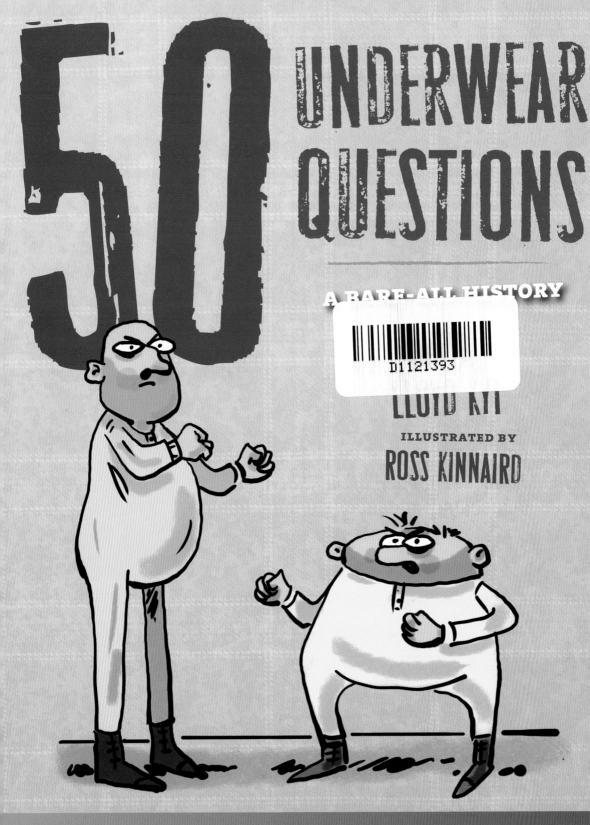

annick press
toronto + new york + vancouver

This book is the third in the 50 Questions series.
Text © 2011 Tanya Lloyd Kyi
Illustrations © 2011 Ross Kinnaird

ANNICK PRESS LTD.

Edited by Catherine Marjoribanks
Copyedited by Gillian Watts
Proofread by Tanya Trafford
Cover and interior design by Irvin Cheung / iCheung Design, inc.
Cover illustration by Ross Kinnaird
Vintage Jockey ad, p 61: Image provided courtesy of Jockey International, Inc. © Jockey International, Inc. Used with Permission.

We acknowledge the support of the Canada Council for the Arts, the Ontario Arts Council, and the Government of Canada through the Canada Book Fund (CBF) for our publishing activities.

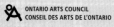

ONTARIO ARTS COUNCIL
CONSEIL DES ARTS DE L'ONTARIO

CATALOGING IN PUBLICATION
Kyi, Tanya Lloyd, 1973-
  50 underwear questions : a bare-all history / Tanya Lloyd Kyi ; illustrated by Ross Kinnaird.

(50 questions series)
Includes bibliographical references and index.
ISBN 978-1-55451-352-9 (pbk.).—ISBN 978-1-55451-353-6 (bound)

   1. Underwear—Juvenile literature. 2. Underwear—History—Juvenile literature. I. Kinnaird, Ross, 1954- II. Title. III. Title: Fifty underwear questions. IV. Series: 50 questions series

GT2073.K95 2011   j391.4'2   C2011-901701-6

Printed and bound in China

Published in the U.S.A. by
Annick Press (U.S.) Ltd.

Distributed in Canada by
Firefly Books Ltd.
66 Leek Crescent
Richmond Hill, ON
L4B 1H1

Distributed in the U.S.A. by
Firefly Books (U.S.) Inc.
P.O. Box 1338
Ellicott Station
Buffalo, NY 14205

Visit our website at **www.annickpress.com**

Visit Tanya Lloyd Kyi at **www.tanyalloydkyi.com**

Acknowledgments

Thanks go to John Cronce and Jockey International for the use of the advertisement that appears on page 61. Also to Catherine Marjoribanks and Gillian Watts, editors extraordinaire, and to designer Irvin Cheung.

TABLE OF CONTENTS

INTRODUCTION
Sneaking a Peek
2

CHAPTER 1
Ancient Undies
4

CHAPTER 2
Underwear Goes Undercover
15

CHAPTER 3
The Cage Stage
28

CHAPTER 4
Unlaced
45

CHAPTER 5
Wartime Wear
62

CHAPTER 6
Rock and Roll and Revolution
78

CHAPTER 7
Underwear Exposé
91

CONCLUSION
All Wrapped Up
103

FURTHER READING 106

BIBLIOGRAPHY 107

INDEX 110

ABOUT THE AUTHOR & ILLUSTRATOR 114

SNEAKiNG A PEEK

START HERE!

WE ALL OWN IT. WE ALL WEAR IT. WE ALL WASH IT. (At least, I hope we do!) So why do we know so little about our underwear? Every morning, we pull on our briefs, boxers, or panties without thinking. We might even assume that we're wearing the same skivvies people have been wearing for centuries. But that's not true!

Underwear was invented way back when cave-dwellers wrapped scraps of leather around their waists. We've come a long way from the loincloths of those ancestors. Since their time, underwear has evolved into something that can straighten, shape, warm, wad, squish, or stuff us. Men have worn tights and garters, breeches and suspenders, Y-fronts and briefs, and even wool full-body suits under their clothes. Women

2

have worn petticoats, crinolines, corsets, bloomers, girdles, bras, and, yes, thongs.

Even though these items are mostly tucked out of sight, they manage to affect the way people walk and the way they work. Around the world, underwear can even reflect the values of societies, symbolizing how people view their bodies and the bodies of others.

The following pages unwrap the answers to all sorts of undercover questions. Each chapter is a sneak peek at a historical period, and all together they form a timeline from the days of saber-toothed tigers to the high-fashion world of modern lingerie—a timeline that stretches through the centuries like a very long piece of waistband elastic.

Chapter 1

ANCIENT UNDIES

When you think of mummified bodies, you might picture their forms wrapped in long, Halloween-style linen strips. Would you believe that underneath their wraps, some mummies are wearing underwear? The preserved bodies of Egyptian pharaohs show us what people of the Mediterranean wore thousands of years ago. And the frozen remains of an ice-age hunter reveal much about primeval European fashion.

It's not easy to trace the history of clothing, because cloth usually disintegrates over time. Along with mummies, scientists study sculptures, paintings, and surviving cultural traditions to help determine what our ancestors wore in the distant past.

Does anyone feel a chill?

IMAGINE YOU'RE HIKING through the Alps and you stumble across . . . a dead body! That's what happened to two German backpackers in 1991. When they found a torso sticking out of the ice, they thought someone had been murdered. They called the police. Soon authorities were on the mountain with jackhammers and ice picks, digging out the "victim."

It turned out there *had* been a murder—the man had been shot with a stone arrow. But no arrests were made. After all, the body was more than 3000 years old!

The iceman had been miraculously preserved by the ice, and he offered researchers all sorts of information about prehistoric underwear. He was dressed in deerskin snow boots, leather-and-fur leggings, and a goatskin loincloth. Sewn together with animal sinew, the loincloth hung from a leather belt at the front, was tucked between his legs, and was attached to the belt at the back.

These items gave scientists information about the climate 3000 years ago, about the technologies known to the iceman's people (sewing, for example), and about the ways early Europeans wore their undies.

Maybe I'm only supposed to wear the fur.

5

What's the latest in loincloths?

Here's a good idea!

THE ICEMAN WASN'T THE ONLY ONE wearing a loincloth. Many ancient societies developed their own variations of leather or cloth worn between the legs and held around the waist. Loincloths were easy to make, they were warm, and they protected sensitive regions from scrapes and prickles.

In some places, such as ancient Egypt, both men and women wore loincloths. In other cultures, women developed their own adaptations. Also, different types were worn in different parts of the world, depending on the climate and the available materials. In North America, some native peoples wore loincloths made from deerskin. Farmers in China wore loincloths made of hemp, while the Inca of South America wore llama wool or animal fur. Mayan men made theirs out of a cloth woven from tree bark.

Styles varied as well. Until the early 1900s, Japanese men wore a long strip of cloth called a *fundoshi*. This was designed to be wrapped around the hips, twisted in the back, then drawn between the legs to tuck into the front waistband, leaving extra cloth to hang over the top like an apron.

Today we might think that loincloths look like ancient boxer-briefs. But they weren't actually worn *underneath* anything—they were more outerwear than underwear. Only in cold climates might a shawl or poncho be added overtop.

SAND IN HIS PANTS

So that's 3000 BCE... 2999 BCE... 2998 BCE...

In ancient Egypt, pharaohs were buried with gold, pets, furniture, and even slaves—everything they might need to live as rich men in the afterlife. In 1352 BCE, the pharaoh Tutankhamen was entombed with 145 loincloths for his future use.

Hopefully Tut's celestial slaves have been doing his laundry. If not, he's only had a pair of clean undies every couple of decades since he died.

Private Part

The *mawashi* worn by modern Japanese sumo wrestlers is a stylized form of loincloth. It's often tied very tightly and sprinkled with water so that it's too slippery for an opponent to grab.

100% Cotton

7

If you see Venus and you see France...?

FOUND IN A CAVE in southern France, the Venus of Lespugue is a rotund figurine depicting an exaggerated woman's body. She was carved from an ivory tusk between 26,000 and 24,000 years ago. And she's wearing underwear.

Well, actually, she's wearing some woven strings around her waist—showing that the people who carved the figurine were some of the first in the world to begin twisting and weaving threads together to form clothing.

The figurine's woven garment is a form of *cache-sexe*. That's a French word for something that hides the genitals. Basically, a cache-sexe is the girl version of a loincloth. Early cache-sexes have been found at a burial site in Denmark, where women from 3000 years ago wore wraparound wool skirts. An excavation in Mali has revealed a layered, fringed belt made of woven tree bark. These kinds of skirts may have been for warmth or for decoration, but anthropologists believe they were also symbols, worn to show that a girl had reached adulthood and was ready to bear children.

P/P
Private Part

In a few ancient civilizations, woman also wore bras. But not the kind of bras we would recognize today. In Rome, women wore bands of cloth or leather wrapped around their breasts, but *outside* their tunics.

100% Cotton

Are loincloths ladylike?

PSST . . . IS THAT GIRL SINGLE? *Is she married? Ask her how old she is. Can you pass her this note and find out where her village is?*

If you were a young man in ancient Papua New Guinea and you had your eye on a particular girl, you wouldn't need all that whispering and note-passing. You could get answers to all your questions just by looking at her *maro*. This rectangular piece of fabric, made from tree bark and elaborately painted and stenciled, was worn around the waist and tied with a belt.

As children, girls ran naked through their villages. When they reached puberty, they received their first *maro*, which covered them from waist to mid-thigh. Each girl received a new, differently painted maro on her wedding night—one she would wear for the rest of her life to mark her status as a married woman.

Today, visitors to Papua New Guinea are more likely to see a maro in the tourist marketplace than wrapped around a woman's waist. The tree-bark fabric has become a symbol of local culture, but the history of the maro stretches far into the ancient past. It's a relative of the loincloths and wraparound skirts worn by women in Polynesia, South America, and Africa.

Private Part

At puberty, an Araweté girl of Brazil is given a wide cotton waistband—a sort of woven belt—to wear under her skirt. She wears this same waistband until her death, just as her ancestors have done for centuries. Because it's considered private, the waistband is rarely taken off. And unlike other Araweté clothing, waistbands aren't handed down to new wearers.

100% Cotton

QUESTION 5

How does a loincloth travel?

"IT's IN THIS MONTH'S *VOGUE!*"

"I saw it on *Entertainment Tonight*!"

"It's what all the trend-watchers are blogging about!"

Today we have magazines, TV shows, and the Internet to bring us the latest fashion trends from around the world. In ancient times, ideas traveled much more slowly. It was more like "Hmmm . . . those foreign sailors at the docks are wearing something strange," or "Have you seen the clothes on those caravan camel-drivers?"

A new loincloth style might take generations to spread just from one side of the Mediterranean to the other. Today, historians are trying to trace how one clothing idea led to the next.

From carvings and paintings, we know that people wore skirt-like loincloths in ancient Egypt. Etruscan people on the north side of the Mediterranean, where Italy is today, probably adapted the Egyptian style. Then the Romans took over. They called their loincloth a *subligaculum*,

but it was basically the same underwear by another name. It was a large, roughly triangular piece of fabric wrapped around the waist, then tucked between the legs and under a belt.

Farmers wore *subligacula* in the fields and gladiators wore them when they fought in the Coliseum. Soldiers wore them underneath knee-length tunics. Even politicians may have worn them underneath their tunics or togas.

P/P

Private Part

Chilly? You could pull on a pair of leg warmers below your *subligaculum*. But only if you were an old man. Otherwise, you'd have to learn to say "fashion faux pas" in ancient Latin.

100% Cotton

Can you battle in those breeches?

Whose stupid idea was this?

PICTURE A BATTLEFIELD.
It's 102 BCE, and the Romans
are stabbing their short swords at an army of Teutonic warriors. There's just one problem with this picture. The Romans are basically battling in dresses—knee-length tunics with a loincloth underneath. The Teutons are leaping around in shirts and shorts.

Who was faster?

In this case, the Romans won the war. But it wasn't because of their dresses! As soon as they got home, in fact, they started wearing shorter tunics. Underneath, they pulled on long, baggy underwear—kind of like coarse brown basketball shorts. This style gave them more freedom to run and fight and ride.

By studying ancient books and artwork, historians can see how these newfangled shorts, known as breeches, slowly spread across Europe. Roman records show that craftspeople were at work making breeches by the fifth century. And eleventh-century illustrations show farmers stripping off their outer clothes in the hot fields and working in their cloth undies. These shorts were tied at the waist with a cord, and also cinched around the upper calves. Medieval knights wore breeches like this under their armor, and aristocrats wore them under their tunics.

PERSIAN PANTS

I wish I had your pants.

Men in Persia may have flaunted divided pants well before their European counterparts. (Just think of Aladdin's puffy silk pants with drawstrings at the ankles.) Some historians suggest that the Romans borrowed this garment idea from the Persians, not the Teutons, and then turned the loose trousers into underpants.

HOW TO DRESS LIKE A GLADIATOR

If your mom or grandma has a large triangular shawl (preferably with tassels), you can try tying your own *subligaculum*.

▶ Spread the shawl behind you, hanging onto two corners and letting the third corner drop toward the floor.
▶ Pull the top two corners around you and tie them at your belly button.
▶ Grab the bottom corner from between your legs and pull it in front of you, tucking it under the knot at your belly button.
▶ Let the extra material hang in front of the knot.
▶ Fasten a belt around your hips to hold your subligaculum in place.
▶ Now all you need to be a gladiator is a coliseum, a weapon, some hungry lions, and a few thousand rabid fans.

Nice Kitty?

Chapter 2

UNDERWEAR GOES UNDERCOVER

Medieval underwear was nothing naughty or worth blushing about. It had two very practical uses: to absorb dirt and to add warmth. But gradually people became more hush-hush about what was hugging their skin. Loincloths stopped flapping in the breeze. Underwear was tucked away, hidden under other layers of clothing.

This was partly because of fabrics and fashion trends, and partly because of new religious attitudes in Europe. "Have you no shame?" cried the new generation of prim church leaders. "Cover up! No flashing allowed!"

Oak leaves? So last year!

Were fig leaves a fashion statement?

IN EARLY MEDIEVAL PAINTINGS, lots of people were portrayed (gasp!) naked. Yup, completely starkers. In the buff. Wearing their birthday suits. Their bodies were on display for the world to see, with no blushing necessary. Even during the early Renaissance, painters such as Michelangelo showed Adam and Eve naked in the Garden of Eden. It wasn't a big deal. After all, out in the fields, farmers were stripping down and working in nothing but a bit of underwear.

Then something changed. A few respected Christian priests began preaching that the human body was impure. After all, the Bible tells us that after they ate the forbidden apple, Adam and Eve were embarrassed by their nakedness, and immediately covered themselves. Obviously, everyone else should do the same! Priests saw the story of Adam and Eve as a message from God that the human body was dirty, immoral, and embarrassing. It should be hidden from sight. And in the early 1500s, the

Roman Catholic priests who met at the Council of Trent made it an official ruling: in all religious art, male and female genitals must be covered up.

Artists began draping robes over their subjects or tucking naked men and women behind shrubbery. When those strategies didn't work, there was always . . . the fig leaf.

Giant, conveniently placed fig leaves began appearing over the private parts of men and women in all sorts of Renaissance paintings and sculptures. Soon people were even painting and gluing fig leaves on historic works, covering up the previously exposed naughty bits.

Were fig leaves underwear? Not really. But they marked a significant step in the way Europeans saw the human body. Private parts were to be hidden beneath underwear, and underwear was to be tucked beneath clothing. If no one saw it and no one talked about it, then everyone could pretend it didn't exist.

The last Judgment. ↓

Phew! The last trousers!

P/P
Private Part

A famous Renaissance painter and sculptor named Daniele da Volterra earned the nickname "Il Braghettone"—the breeches maker—after he was hired to paint clothes on the naked people in Michelangelo's *Last Judgment*.

100% Cotton

QUESTION 8
What's that smell?

HAVE YOU EVER SEEN a medieval European village in a film or cartoon? The sort of picturesque place that was home to Belle and Gaston in Disney's *Beauty and the Beast*? Well, the milkmaids and hunters living in those thatched cottages smelled nothing like roses.

The truth is, they didn't bathe.

In many parts of Europe, people thought bathing would make you sick. After the plague killed millions of people in the 1300s, "unsanitary" baths and steam rooms got blamed for the disease. People might—*might*—wash their faces and hands after a particularly hard day of work. But climb into a bathtub? That was unthinkable!

To stay even remotely clean, they relied on their underwear. In the Middle Ages, people in most parts of Europe wore shifts, which were long shirts. Men wore breeches on their bottom halves. Depending on where they lived, women wore similar breeches or left their bottoms bare and wore petticoats—simple underskirts—as underwear.

Whatever the style, undies helped to soak up sweat and absorb dirt. Best of all, they were easily laundered. Because people weren't bathing, they were tormented by lice and fleas. Scrubbing their underwear could wash away the week's collection of creepy-crawlies.

king

King's Undies

SCRUB UNDERWEAR WITH PEBBLES OR BEAT IT ON ROCKS.

SOAK IT IN PEE FROM THE CHAMBER POT— THE ACID WILL HELP DISSOLVE THE DIRT.

ADD HERBS TO COVER UP THE PEE SMELL.

PRESTO! PERFECTLY CLEAN!

Villagers would probably have owned a couple of pairs of breeches-style underwear woven from hemp. Rich people had their underclothes made from linen. Notes from France in the 1600s say that Louis XIV changed his linen underwear every day and every night, and his skin was rubbed with scented linen cloths between changes.

Without a bath, that was as clean as a king could get.

QUESTION 9

Can you strip to say "sorry"?

THE MEDIEVAL MAN'S GUIDE TO ETIQUETTE

Need to apologize? Want to show people that you're a good and decent guy? A real man shows his humility by stripping down to his underwear. In public. No matter the weather.

Note: *You might want to consider the effects of offensive body odor on the above method of apology. If you have chosen not to bathe for several months, and you strip to your undershirt in public, you do so at your own risk.*

IN THE 13TH CENTURY, a man might dress in his underwear in public to show that he was humble, that he had nothing to hide, that he didn't value material possessions. One man who had this goal in mind when he stripped to his skivvies was Jean de Joinville. Born about 1224, he was a French noble and writer who went to the Middle East with the religious Crusades. To prove that he was truly faithful—not just another stuck-up "I went on a Crusade and you didn't" kind of snob—he traveled all the way wearing nothing but underwear.

P/P
Private Part

Most medieval laundry was done on the riverbank. People either washed their own skivvies or hired a local washerwoman to do their laundry—except in the case of some monks and priests. These men thought it might be improper for a woman to see their underwear, so they hired washer*men* instead.

100% Cotton

In 1077, Henry IV, the King of Germany and Holy Roman Emperor, felt the need to apologize to Pope Gregory VII after a particularly nasty battle over papal powers. The Pope had threatened to excommunicate Henry, and Henry had threatened to depose the Pope. To mend fences, Henry followed His Holiness to a castle high in the Italian Alps. The king knelt outside in the icy wind and stripped down to his long, nightgown-like undershirt to prove his humility. He stayed there for three days, until the Pope was convinced of his sincerity and granted forgiveness.

Sometimes the Church *made* people show their underwear, as a sort of chastisement or penance. Medieval records speak of women having to stand in church wearing only their long woven undershirts, as punishment for being unfaithful to their husbands. Members of a Catholic offshoot group called the Lollards also had to repent their wrongdoings while wearing only their undies.

Today we see these punishments as another sign that underwear was slowly becoming something to be embarrassed about. People no longer thought it was normal—let alone fun—to stand around in their skivvies.

THE UNSANITARY SIEGE

"Darling, I love you. And to show my support, I'm not going to change my underwear until we win this battle!"

That's basically what Princess Isabella of Spain said in 1601 when she and her husband, Albert, laid siege to the city of Ostend (in present-day Belgium), which was then being held by the Dutch. They tried to force the Dutch to surrender by surrounding the city and limiting its food supply.

Unfortunately for Isabella, this was one of the longest sieges in history—it lasted for three years. By the time it was over, the princess's lovely chemise was far from white, definitely not sweet-smelling, and certainly not fit to be seen!

A KNIGHT IN SHINING ARMOR: the ultimate rescue service, and the dream of every princess imprisoned in a castle tower.

As long as the situation wasn't urgent.

Any princess who sent a distress text to rescueme@chivalry.com in the 1300s would have had a long wait. It could take knights more than an hour just to get dressed!

First a knight donned his *gambeson*, or quilted underwear. This thigh-length coat, made of linen or wool, absorbed sweat, offered extra protection against blows, and, most important, kept his chain mail from chafing.

Made of hundreds of linked metal rings, chain mail was designed to keep lances and swords from piercing the skin. A heavier, solid metal armor called plate mail could also be worn. It did an even better job of protecting knights from arrows.

All this metal was also a kind of underwear, because overtop it knights wore yet another layer, a tunic, to keep the metal from growing hot in the blazing sun.

Not only did a knight take a long time to get dressed, he couldn't do it on his own. His armor weighed up to 23 kilograms (50 pounds), so he needed a squire to help lift it into place.

Rather than waiting for this knight in shining armor to finally ride up on his white horse, the princess would probably be better off if she rescued herself!

QUESTION 10

Squire, where are my skivvies?

PLS SND HLP + DBL PPRONI PIZZA

What's under that kimono?

NETTLES, BAMBOO, AND SILK: these were all underwear fabrics in different parts of Asia.

In Japan, where fashion and modesty dictated that men and women wrap themselves in several layers of fabric, people found it hard to keep cool during the long, humid summers. They came up with a lightweight blend of cotton and a fiber called ramie, made from nettle plants. While nettles sting and are generally best avoided in the garden, nettle fibers are hollow, and so the fabric was naturally insulating—cool in summer, warm in winter. This filmy material was made into summer under-robes for women and underpants for men. Unfortunately, the women still had to wrap up in other layers below and beneath. Men were able to wander around in their undies if they pleased.

Ramie was also used in Chinese clothing, or people could wear undershirts made of thinly sliced and woven bamboo. They sometimes even tied tiny bamboo tubes under their clothes. Ancient Asia had the same nagging problem with fleas that non-bathing medieval Europe did. But with a dab of syrup at one end, these small bamboo sticks became an ideal trap. The sweetness tempted the creatures

Nettle undies. The first prototype.

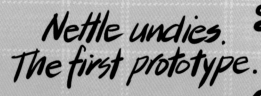

down the tube, and the bug-filled bamboo could be thrown away at the end of the day.

If the times called for fighting rather than flea-chasing, Chinese men donned silk under-armor. Historians know that the soldiers of Genghis Khan chose this tightly woven fabric because it would catch at an arrow point, slowing it down as it pierced the body. Then, by carefully tugging on the silk, the men could more easily draw the arrow from the wound.

CHANGE YOUR PANTS, CHANGE THE WORLD

As far-flung parts of the world grew more closely connected in the late 1800s and early 1900s, leaders in places such as Japan and Turkey actively encouraged their people to abandon traditional costumes and start dressing like Europeans. They wanted their countries to be progressive and technologically advanced, and to them, European dress seemed more modern.

Put some clothes on—
you look ridiculous!

Who put the Europeans in charge?

ON THE ISLANDS OF POLYNESIA, people wore little or no clothing until the 1700s, when European missionaries sailed in and sputtered, "Cover yourselves! You're practically naked!"

As we know from their fussing with fig leaves, Europeans now believed that bodies should be covered. As they began exploring the oceans, they shipped their prim opinions around the world. The arrival of Christian missionaries, who had strict ideas about proper dress, changed underwear fashions in places from Tahiti to Florida.

Missionaries in North America asked native peoples to change their faith ... "And, while you're at it, change into Western clothes!" Travelers in Nigeria were appalled to see children running around naked, so they ordered tops and bottoms for everyone. Finnish missionaries arrived in Namibia in the 1800s, condemned leather loincloths and other traditional clothing, and taught the people to sew cotton dresses and shirts.

With all this traveling and colonizing and adapting going on, loincloths finally made their way out of the fashion closet and into the museum.

HAVE YOU HEARD THIS ONE?

Knock knock!

Knock knock.
Who's there?
Icy.
Icy who?
Icy your underwear!

Because it's not polite to talk about our underwear in public, it's the perfect subject for jokes and riddles. Can you create your own underwear joke? To gather ideas, think of all the different words we use: loincloths, ginch, gonch, skivvies, panties, boxers, briefs, bras ... What sorts of puns or silly questions can you create?

Q. What did the busy executive say to the underwear sales clerk?
A. Keep it brief.

Now I look really fashionable.

Chapter 3
THE CAGE STAGE

A few hundred years ago, people laced their corsets so tightly they couldn't breathe, women's underskirts were too wide to fit through doorways, and men carried keys and coins in their crotches!

In this age of extremes, people developed strange views about the human body. They believed women should have impossibly tiny waists, and that men should have large calves and attention-getting crotches. To achieve these shapes, everyone depended on a wild assortment of underwear. Sometimes getting into one's undies was a bit like climbing into a prison cell.

Where can I get those calves?

In the 1520s, men didn't wear suits to palace balls—they wore long, decorated shirts called doublets. Originally adapted from undershirts, such as the quilted gambeson worn by a knight, doublets were waist- or hip-length in the 1400s. By the time the 1500s rolled around, though, men were wearing thigh-length versions. Underneath, they wore tights.

Beneath the thin covering of his tights, the calves of the English king, Henry VIII, were visibly large and strong. It wasn't long before other men in his court made the connection. Henry attracted masses of women . . . and he had massive calves. Obviously, women loved big calves! Soon the market was flooded with false-calf pads. Held in place by a belt that wrapped around the shin, they looked like modern soccer pads worn backwards. These were strapped on under a man's tights to present a leg muscle that—apparently—no woman could resist.

I keep cod in mine.

How do you cover the royal jewels?

BECAUSE TIGHTS WERE THIN and doublets were short, in 16th-century Europe a fashionable man's private parts could sometimes become uncomfortably . . . noticeable. A gentleman's tights were actually individual leggings, not sewn together at the crotch or the waist. So, to avoid flashing the court, men strapped on codpieces—fabric pouches that fitted over the crotch of their tights. At the time, *cod* was a name (not a very polite one) used for part of a man's privates.

As time passed and the fashion became more popular, codpieces grew larger . . . and larger . . . and larger! Many men stuffed their private regions with fabric in an effort to look more manly and powerful. Soon, codpieces even came equipped with pockets, which were useful for carrying loose coins or tobacco. King Henry VIII's codpiece had so much storage space and stuffing that it became regally large and eye-catching—which was undoubtedly the whole point!

With the king leading the fashion charge, tights and codpieces became the underwear of choice for courtly men, and things stayed that way for most of the 1500s.

CULTURE SHOCK

When Nasir al-Din Shah, King of Persia, visited Europe in 1873, he was shocked by the women's low-cut dresses and exposed cleavage. He said that even the women in his harem dressed more modestly. Misled by the bustle-enhanced skirts that ballooned over ladies' bottoms, the king assumed that European women wore so little on top and so much on their lower halves because their bodies must be seriously deformed.

Give us a kiss.

Does this make my bottom look big... enough?

SILK, VELVET, TAFFETA, SATIN, AND BROCADE—these were the fabrics that arrived on 16th-century ships from the Middle East and Asia. In the courts of Europe, women were crazy for them.

But how to show them off? How to make sure everyone noticed the pattern, the sheen . . . the expense?

Introducing—the farthingale.

The farthingale was an underskirt constructed with hoops made of cane. The hoops helped the top skirt stand out, curving it outward from the waist like a bell. The first and narrowest hoop sat just below the hips, so it was easy for a woman to grab and adjust as she sat down. (Sitting down in a farthingale was quite an acrobatic feat, but comfort wasn't the main goal.) Below the hips, the hoops grew wider and wider. The largest one circled the ankles, just high enough off the floor to prevent tripping.

Worn with at least one petticoat underneath, this contraption held a skirt's fabric away from the waist and let it sweep elegantly to the floor, making sure that people could both admire and envy it.

ROCK-STAR ROYALS

Paparazzi 1751

Early fashion trends were often led by kings, queens, and aristocrats. Like today's rock stars, they had access to the newest fabrics and the best tailors. They traveled more than other people and picked up ideas from neighboring countries. They could also afford to buy new linens every week or replace their undershirts every time they grew dirty.

In Europe, lower-class women who wanted to imitate the full-skirted styles of society ladies wore "bum rolls"—thick sausages of fabric tied around the hips to hold the material of their dresses away from their bodies. And men who wanted to look posh started decorating the edges of their undershirts. This move annoyed the upper classes so much that London passed a law: bejeweled undershirts could be worn only by the gentry.

Can you cinch it any tighter?

uh-oh!

WHEN CATHERINE DE' MEDICI, wife of King Henry II of France, declared that women's waists should be tiny, every female in France started sucking in her gut. The standard for beauty was a waist no bigger than Catherine's 13 inches (33 centimeters)—small enough that your hands could meet around your midsection. Soon ladies across 16th-century Europe were visiting their clothiers to order new corsets.

Usually made of thick linen, corsets stretched from under the arms to the top of the hips. They were strengthened with strips of cane. Or bone. Or metal. Oh, and they were equipped with laces at the back, so a lady's maid could haul away on them until the corset was cinched as tightly as possible. Wearing one of these contraptions could give even a slightly overweight woman an hourglass figure.

At a typical ball, every lady would appear as sculpted as possible. A busk—a flat piece of wood or metal inserted in the front of the corset—would give her impeccable posture and hide any wrinkles in the chemise underneath. Strips of whalebone along the sides and back would elongate her figure and narrow her waist, while laces in the back allowed the entire corset to be cinched as tightly as possible.

The idea of corsets was hardly new. They had been worn by women all over the world and through the centuries. In fact, they were worn by both men and women in Crete around 2000 BCE. At that time they served as outerwear, not underwear, and they weren't laced so tightly. But thanks to the preferences of Catherine de' Medici and other high-society women, constricting corsets became the "must-have" fashion of the 16th century, and they remained in vogue for more than 200 years.

Private Part

As time went by, royal tailors "improved" the farthingale by replacing the cane hoops with rings of whalebone. In the 1800s, whalebone, also known as baleen, was used in everything from umbrellas to riding whips. For women it offered a more expensive but stronger alternative to cane—if you didn't mind wearing baleen around your backside. Anything for fashion.

100% Cotton

LACES ARE FOR LADiES

Peasant women in Catherine's time continued to wear basic chemises, or undershirts, possibly with a very loose corset overtop. A restrictive corset wouldn't have allowed them to mop the floors, stoke the fire, or cook the meals. How could they have raised their children if they couldn't bend . . . or breathe? In the privacy of their own homes, even noblewomen and the wives of wealthy landowners and merchants probably fastened their corsets quite loosely for greater comfort.

QUESTION 17

Isn't that just dandy?

I think I look dandy!

SUCK IN THAT BELLY! It wasn't just women who were squeezing themselves into corsets. In the early 1800s, men also laced up—led by an English playboy named Beau Brummell.

Known as "dandies," Beau and his friends wore chest-to-hip corsets that created an abnormally narrow shape. They sauntered around London in suits and ties, introducing yet another menswear style. And, according to Beau, it was best to finish off an outfit with gleaming black boots, preferably polished with champagne. Men who wanted a less extreme version of the dandy look asked their tailors for more moderate waist-cinchers.

The popularity of corsets for men quickly faded in the early 1800s, only to pop up again a hundred years later, when narrow suit jackets came back into fashion. There was no hiding a pot belly beneath one of those sleek suits, so men donned restrictive underwear once more.

Even today there's an English corset-maker, known as Mr. Pearl, who wears an 18-inch corset himself and designs custom cages for others.

QUESTION 18

Were petticoats posh?

Oops! 15 cups of tea. Now I need to pee.

CORSETS AND FARTHINGALES were meant for the privileged, for women who could sit around and drink tea all day. Petticoats, on the other hand— simple, loose, easy-to-wash underskirts—were for everyone. Rich or poor, noble or peasant, hausfrau in Germany or colonist in India—everyone wore them.

This was the most versatile underwear of the 16th to 19th centuries. A light petticoat would protect the material of a fancy dress from sweat and body odor. It would keep a girl properly covered if she happened to trip on the street. A quilted petticoat offered extra warmth in winter. And a lacy petticoat could be allowed to peek out from under a fancy open-skirted gown for an added layer of decoration.

Best of all, wearing a petticoat helped to hold a woman's skirt out from her body. By creating this illusion of larger hips—though not as exaggerated as the effect of corsets and farthingales—women hoped to show off their slim waists.

Of course, if a light petticoat could make the waist look better, wouldn't a wider, heavier petticoat make it look its best? That's the question that led to the fashion craze of the 1700s—panniers.

SHE'S PACKING PANNIERS

By the 1730s, the "in" look in Europe was a figure with a flat front and rounded sides. To create this silhouette, aristocratic women wore petticoats that were reinforced at the hips with something called *panniers*. Basically they were wearing upside-down baskets around their waists.

As time passed, the reinforcements grew. And grew. By the 1740s, women's skirts were incredibly wide—wider than their arms could reach. Now panniers had to be made with hinges. When a woman needed to pass through a doorway, she would fold the metal or wooden "baskets" up under her armpits, holding them there until the doorway had been safely navigated.

Rats!

P/P

Private Part

A proper woman always wore a padded petticoat between her hoops and her dress, to hide the lines of the hoops from view. Women who let their hoops show through were considered uncouth.

100% Cotton

DON'T RUB THAT ROBE

Japanese men and women traditionally wore a *nagajuban*, or under-robe, beneath their elaborate kimonos, for much the same reason that European women always wore petticoats under their gowns. Expensive silks and brocades were difficult to wash, but if the lighter under-robe got sweaty, it could be easily laundered or replaced.

QUESTION 19

Who got cagey with crinolines?

IT'S AN AGE-OLD PROBLEM: how can the average woman keep up with aristocratic fashion trends? By the 1850s, women who wanted to mimic fine ladies' show-offy giant hooped skirts were wearing at least three—and sometimes as many as six—heavily starched petticoats to puff up their best frocks. That much underwear was a drag to drag around!

Then an American named W. S. Thomson came to the rescue with his new invention: the metal cage crinoline. This modern version of the farthingale was shaped like a dome instead of the older-style bell. It used thin steel bands to support an underskirt that would hold top skirts away from the legs. Most important, it was lighter

Blacksmith ~~Blacksmith~~ *Tailor*

and cheaper than the original farthingale, and designed to be useful and available to pretty much everyone.

Steel underwear! To women who had always wanted to look like aristocrats, it was a revelation. To wear an afternoon dress, a woman might choose a smaller crinoline, with only 9 or 10 hoops. For underneath a ball gown, she would want the added support and wider effect of up to 18 hoops.

Of course, the fledgling crinoline-wearer had to learn new rules for movement. When she sat down (preferably on a specially designed armless chair with extra room at the back), she had to carefully hold down and smooth out her skirt. Otherwise, the entire cage might pop up in front to reveal her legs. And she had to be especially careful on windy days, when a sudden gust could catch the fabric of her skirt and turn it sideways, giving passing men a scandalous view of her ankles and calves.

(P/P) Private Part

The 1840s brought some cold winters. The 1850s brought the cage crinoline, and fewer petticoats to protect a woman's bottom from the icy wind. Together, these things convinced women in England and North America to start wearing drawers. Until then, many had gone bare-bottomed under their skirts.

100% Cotton

PUMP IT UP

Phut!

The cage crinoline wasn't the first attempt to get women out of their piles of petticoats.

An inventor in 1856 patented an inflatable underskirt, kind of like a bicycle tire meant to be worn as underwear. By blowing into a hose or attaching bellows, a woman could pump enough air into the rubber tubes in her underskirt to lift her dress as if she were wearing several layers of cloth. But imagine the sound it would make if she sprang a leak!

Mmm! What's cooking, Mom?

What causes a crinoline crisis?

THERE WERE A FEW PROBLEMS with the cage crinoline trend. Now everyone—everyone!—was wearing enormous hoops. The huge skirts, combined with the flammable dress materials of the time, made for an instant fire hazard. While an aristocrat on her way to a ball might be relatively safe, a mother preparing dinner over the kitchen fire was taking her life in her hands.

In London in 1863, two women were burned to death when their skirts brushed against fire grates. In Manchester, England, a young woman was passing by the kitchen fire when her crinoline bumped a kettle. The boiling contents scalded and killed a child.

Across Europe and North America, crinolines led to hundreds of injuries and deaths. Did the list of horrible accidents convince women to wear smaller skirts? Well, no. Apparently fashion was worth the small risk of death by fire.

P/P

Private Part

A bustle was a frame that puffed out the back of a woman's dress. When England celebrated Queen Victoria's Golden Jubilee in 1887, one clothing company released a special-edition bustle containing a music box that played "God Save the Queen" whenever the wearer sat down. History does not record whether or not the Queen was "amused."

100% Cotton

CAGED IN A CRINOLINE

Would you be happy in 19th-century underwear?
Try this experiment to find out:

What you'll need:
- A hula hoop
- Five or six long ribbons
- Jeans or pants with belt loops

What to do:
1. Kneel in the center of the hula hoop.
2. Using the ribbons, tie each of your belt loops to the hoop.

Now you're dressed like a lady of the 1800s. Try walking around your house. Do you fit through the doorways? Can you reach the counter to make yourself a sandwich? Can you sit on the couch? What parts of your life would have to change if you dressed in a gown and crinoline every day?

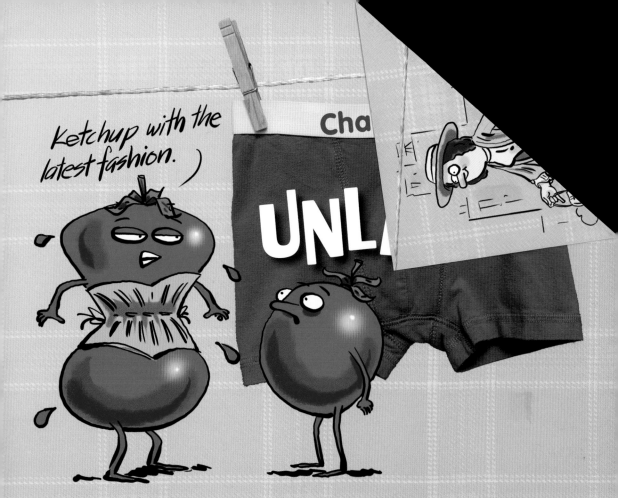

Ketchup with the latest fashion.

Cha

UNL

In the late 1800s and early 1900s, people began questioning their underwear options. Could women possibly be freed from dragging around those long, layered petticoats and awkward hooped crinolines? Was it really necessary to wear a tightly cinched corset that squeezed one's internal organs like a ripe tomato? And men wondered whether wearing more, or different, underwear could make them healthier and more robust.

Companies in Europe and North America were quick to answer: "Yes! Step right up and we'll sell you a new and better product!"

Was it a bloomin' bright idea?

"**WHAT ARE THOSE WOMEN WEARING?** They're practically naked!"

People gasped and pointed.

Actually, Amelia Bloomer and her two friends were completely covered as they strolled down the streets of a New York town in 1851. But instead of ankle-length skirts, they wore (oh my!) long *pantaloons* with short skirts overtop.

It had all started quite innocently, when Amelia began writing letters to her local paper, wondering why women had to wear floor-length dresses while men could wander the world in pants. Why the double standard? Shortly after, two Elizabeths came knocking at Amelia's door. They were cousins: Elizabeth Cady Stanton and Elizabeth Smith Miller. They had an idea, and they thought Amelia might like it. They'd been designing their idea of the perfect daywear for modern women. Basing their creations on loose Turkish trousers, they had sewn pairs of cotton pantaloons that flared modestly around the legs, then gathered neatly at the ankles.

Soon Amelia and the Elizabeths were showing off their designs in public . . . and shocking the country in the process. News of the scandal spread. Before long, journalists had nicknamed the new ankle-length pants "bloomers," in Amelia Bloomer's honor.

Why the bother about bloomers?

WHEN THE PEOPLE of 19th-century New York saw Amelia and the Elizabeths in their short skirts and pantaloons, it was as if a group of lingerie models had suddenly left their catalogue pages and gone skipping through downtown in their underwear. People just weren't used to seeing women without floor-length skirts . . . *ever!*

The costume raised all sorts of questions:

- If women are willing to wear their underwear in public or appear in divided pants like men, what else might they do?

- What if women are so influenced by wearing bloomers that they start thinking and speaking like men?

- What if women start drinking in pubs and leave their babies to be cared for by their husbands?

- What if these newfangled bloomers completely destroy decent American society?

On the other hand, activists immediately adopted bloomers and regularly wore them at public events, making "freedom dress" the official clothing of the women's rights movement across the United States. Women should be allowed to vote, the suffragettes cried. And they should be allowed to wear their bloomers to the polls!

BLOOMERS ON BIKES

Amelia Bloomer didn't convince all women to stop wearing skirts. Her ideas were just too radical for her time—after all, in England, the notoriously prudish Queen Victoria was still on the throne. But bloomers became the sportswear of choice for female athletes, especially when cycling became a popular hobby in the 1870s and 1880s. No room for hooped skirts or cumbersome petticoats on a bicycle! Tennis players and gymnasts also found bloomers very liberating. After all, it isn't easy—or modest—to perform a handstand when your skirt flips over your head every time you try.

QUESTION 23

What were they thinking?

IN 1881, A GROUP OF WOMEN in London, England, came up with some startling ideas:

PUTTING ON UNDERWEAR SHOULD NOT FEEL LIKE TYING A HEAVY SACK OF FLOUR AROUND YOUR WAIST.

UNDERWEAR SHOULD NOT WARP YOUR RIBS OR SQUISH YOUR KIDNEYS.

YOU SHOULD BE ABLE TO MOVE AROUND. AND YOU SHOULD BE ABLE TO WEAR UNDERWEAR— AT THE SAME TIME!

These women, under the banner of the Rational Dress Society, suggested styles such as bloomers, loose undershirts, and combination drawer-and-undershirt garments. Their idea that women should wear no more than 3 kilograms (7 pounds) of underwear would cut its average weight in half.

These ideas seem like common sense today, but in the late 1800s, respectable women were still rather tight-laced—literally.

Who won the next round?

A JAB, AN UNDERCUT, A RIGHT HOOK ... and long johns won the day.

Fighter John L. Sullivan was born in Massachusetts in 1858 and took up boxing at a time when it was still done with bare fists. His matches could last for hours—this guy was tough. And when John, the Boston Strong Boy and heavyweight champion, stepped into the ring, men across North America wanted to look just like him.

While most boxers wore knee-length drawers, John fought in a pair of ankle-length woolen leggings. Men quickly adopted the style and named them "long johns," after their hero.

Unless you were a boxer, though, your long johns were worn as warm, woolly, ankle-length underpants, designed to keep you cozy even on the coldest winter days. Women wore them, too. And while other undie choices eventually fell by the wayside, long johns have hung in for the whole 10 rounds. Today they're even available in high-tech fabrics for outdoor workers and sports enthusiasts.

Long John.
→

Short John.
↙

50

skritch

scratch

(P/P) Private Part

Some boxing fans have suggested that wearing his hot, itchy wool pants in the ring is what gave John L. Sullivan his fighting spirit.

100% Cotton

EUR 110/116 US 4–6Y
CA 4–6A CN 120/60

BURLAP BOTTOMS

In the late 1800s, poor families often couldn't afford the extra fabric needed for children's underwear. Inventive mothers began saving the burlap sacks from their flour and rice purchases, boiling the material until it softened, then sewing it into shorts. There was only one problem—the brand names didn't always boil off the burlap. Youngsters, and even a few adults, had to walk around with "ACME Flour" stamped on their behinds. How embarrassing!

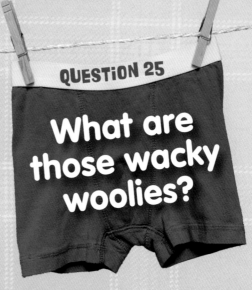

What are those wacky woolies?

ONE DAY A LONDON BUSINESSMAN named Lewis Tomalin happened to read a book by a German zoologist and physiologist named Dr. Gustav Jaeger—and the whole world of underwear changed.

Gustav believed that wool was the perfect natural fabric. He claimed that by dressing entirely in wool, he had lost weight, gained strength, and improved his singing voice. Once he'd read Gustav's book, Lewis was convinced as well. He built a giant bonfire in the backyard and burned every non-woolen piece of clothing in his household. Then Lewis made a deal with the author, started his own business under Gustav's name, and began making all-wool under-wear as fast as he could. In 1884, Lewis opened a shop on one of London's fashionable streets, hanging up a sign that proclaimed: "Dr. Jaeger's Sanitary Woollen System."

La La La

52

Lewis's first product was a kind of beige under-suit for men that was free of artificial fabrics and dyes. It had a high neck, long sleeves, and a double layer of cloth over the chest—like a thick, full-body version of today's long johns. And so the wool union suit was born, a "union" of underpants and undershirt.

By the early 1900s there were 20 Jaeger stores in Britain, and the company was expanding to include other natural, and presumably healthy, fabrics such as angora and cashmere. They even made camel-hair underwear!

DR. JAEGER'S GUIDE TO GOOD HEALTH

WEARING COTTON OR LINEN MAKES YOU SICK.

ANIMAL-BASED FIBERS ALLOW THE BODY'S TOXINS TO ESCAPE.

THE BEST ANIMAL-BASED PRODUCT OF ALL: WOOL!

It's not baad!

 Private Part

Modern scientists have found no evidence to support Dr. Jaeger's claims that wool boosts people's strength. It may keep wearers toasty warm, but it doesn't make them any healthier.

100% Cotton

OLD IDEAS

Cool!

The Inuit of northern Canada were experts in one-piece under-wear long before Lewis Tomalin. They, too, had a preference for animal-based fabrics, probably because it's hard to grow cotton—or anything else—in the Arctic. In winter, hunters wore an *attigi*, an inner garment made of caribou skin, worn with the hair facing toward the body. Over it they wore an outer garment of cari-bou skin (with the hair facing out) called a *qulittaq*. Babies were dressed in one-piece caribou-skin "union suits" to keep their skin completely protected from the Arctic cold.

Can you actually freeze your fanny off?

IN THE EARLY 1900s, North American farmers often wore union suits. They pulled on the thick, full-body long underwear in the fall and left it on until spring, when it was finally time for a bath.

Sounds a bit stinky, doesn't it? But would *you* want to strip to your skin in midwinter, before the days of furnaces and hot water heaters? Probably not! Even the cleanest of clean freaks bathed only once a week.

This presented a challenge to the underwear manufacturers. With all this wearing and so little washing, how would their products hold up? If the suits were going to be worn for weeks or months at a time, they needed extra-strength stitching, amazing shape-holding power, and . . . oh yes, some way to allow men to use the bathroom.

In search of less bulky underwear solutions, the companies first offered union suits with no crotch openings.

The customers said, "Strip off the entire suit just to go to the bathroom? No, thanks."

Next, companies tried button-up flaps over the bottoms of the suits.

The customers said, "A bit better, but try to fasten two buttons behind our back with cold fingers in the middle of the night? We don't think so."

Finally the companies tried an open flap.

The customers said, "Do we feel a draft? And why is this flap falling down to chafe our backsides?"

Baffled companies everywhere were scratching their heads.

It can't be bath time yet. It's only March!

55

QUESTION 27

Who can make a better backside?

Next time, get your bright ideas in daytime!

BUTTONING, DROOPING, AND CHAFING. These were problems that gave Horace Greeley Johnson bad dreams—literally.

Horace grew up surrounded by underwear. His father owned a knitting mill in Ontario, where Horace started working at the age of 16. In 1901 he moved on to the Cooper Underwear Company in Kenosha, Wisconsin. There, he and other designers struggled with the major problems of modern underwear.

Then Horace woke up with a middle-of-the-night inspiration. Floating in the darkness above him, he could see the perfect union-suit design. Worried that he would forget the idea by morning, he woke his wife and asked her to sew a sample from scrap material.

By 1910, Horace and the owner of the Cooper Company had patented the Kenosha Klosed Krotch union suit. A diagonal flap between the legs allowed the crotch of the underwear to stay closed during normal wear, but it could be easily pulled apart for bathroom needs. The design quickly caught on with workers across the country, and the Cooper Company's business boomed.

"Klosed Krotch" Johnson made enough money to buy his own mansion, send his nephews to college, and travel across the country in his own car. And several decades later, the Cooper Underwear Company became the first producers of men's briefs.

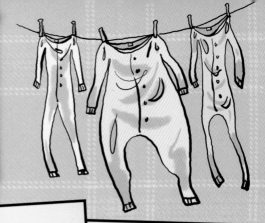

P/P Private Part

Even the most stretchy union suits couldn't expand to fit all sizes. Some underwear companies offered specially cut suits with extra belly room, designed for "stout" men.

100% Cotton

HOLDING IT TOGETHER

UNDERWEAR GOES ON AND UNDERWEAR COMES OFF. IN BETWEEN, WHAT HOLDS IT ALL TOGETHER?

2000 BCE

THE FIRST BUTTONS WERE CREATED IN PERSIA, GREECE, AND EGYPT. THEY WERE PROBABLY USED DECORATIVELY, LIKE BEADS.

700 CE

BUTTONS WERE USED TO HOLD TOGETHER CLOAKS AND SLEEVE CUFFS, BUT DRAWSTRINGS AND RIBBONS WERE THE PREFERRED CLOSERS FOR MEN'S AND WOMEN'S UNDERWEAR.

1820

BRITISH INVENTOR THOMAS HANCOCK SLICED RUBBER SCRAPS INTO THIN STRIPS, THEN STUCK THE STRIPS ONTO FABRIC TO MAKE THE FIRST ELASTIC WEBBING. THERE WERE A FEW PROBLEMS. IT WAS STICKY, IT GOT SMELLY WHEN MIXED WITH A LITTLE BODY HEAT, AND . . . UH-OH, IT DIDN'T LAST LONG. HANG ON TO YOUR UNDERPANTS!

1700s

PEOPLE HELD THEIR GARTERS AND SOMETIMES THEIR WAISTBANDS IN PLACE WITH SMALL BRASS SPRINGS. OUCH! SPRINGS PINCHED!

1836

CHARLES GOODYEAR (YUP, THEY NAMED A TIRE COMPANY AFTER HIM) THREW SOME RUBBER, SULFUR, AND WHITE LEAD ON THE STOVE AND FOUND THAT HE HAD A FORMULA FOR RUBBER THAT DIDN'T DISINTEGRATE. EXCEPT MAYBE IN HOT PLACES. SUCH AS LAUNDRY TUBS. BACK TO THE DRAWING BOARD!

Underwear
Research and Development

1925

THE DUNLOP RUBBER COMPANY CREATED RUBBER ELASTIC THAT COULD ACTUALLY BE BOILED. UNDERWEAR WEARERS OF THE WORLD COULD FINALLY WASH THEIR KNICKERS IN HOT WATER!

How do you courier the family jewels?

HELP WANTED

Bike Jockey — *As one of the city's elite bicycle couriers, you will race through the bumpy streets of Boston to deliver urgent packages. Only those with especially durable crotches need apply.*

IN THE LATE 1800s, Boston's streets were paved with cobblestones. Balancing one's crotch on a hard leather bike seat while swerving along the world's bumpiest roads was just not comfortable! By the end of a long day, some bike jockeys were feeling numb in their nether regions.

A Chicago sports store worker, C. F. Bennett, heard about the cyclists' problems in Boston and came up with an innovative solution. He designed a padded strap, held in place with wide bands of elastic, that could be worn to support the rider's vulnerable anatomy.

Bennett's protector was so popular that in 1897 he patented the idea and started his own business, the Bike Web Company. He called his product the "jockey strap" in honor of the bike jockeys—a name that was quickly shortened to "jock strap." The contraption grew popular with other sports enthusiasts, too. Soon even high school athletes were wearing them, which is how they earned the nickname "jocks."

P/P
Private Part

The "jill strap" (or "jill") was created once women started competing in contact sports such as hockey, rugby, and martial arts. Like the jock, the jill protects the groin with a fabric pad or plastic cup.

100% Cotton

A SHOCK TO THE SYSTEM

This will help you sleep, sir.

Bladder problems? Can't sleep? According to catalogue advertisements in 1900, you could cure all these problems and more by wearing a modified jock strap called the Heidelberg Electric Belt, available for the low, low price of $4. This battery-powered device sent a shock of electric current to the groin every few seconds and was meant to stimulate nerve function and circulation. In reality, it guaranteed nothing but pain.

Who needs new undies?

IN THE EARLY 1900s, all sorts of companies were interested in men's underwear. There were 50 different underwear makers in the United States and Britain alone. Companies such as Fruit of the Loom were eagerly looking for new ways to advertise their products. There was even a magazine called *MAN and His Clothes*, in which writers speculated about the future of men's underwear fashion.

There was just one problem: men didn't care.

The average man was used to his union suit. It was comfortable. It was warm. Why bother with new underwear?

To attract customers, underwear companies used two strategies. Some associated their products with better health, just as Lewis Tomalin had done with his first woolen union suits. Other companies created advertisements to link underwear with athleticism and attractiveness. For the first time, some men began to wonder . . . Were women looking at their undies? Maybe better undies would attract . . . more girls?

Slowly, young men began buying new and more interesting styles of underwear. Shorts now came in colors such as baby blue, pale pink, and minty green—apparently, the perfect shades to make one better at sports . . . and dating.

THE MEDIA MESSAGE

Check out this vintage advertisement for a man's union suit. In the early 1900s, advertisers were eager to reach their customers with messages of health, strength, and adventure. What signals is this advertiser sending? What do these images seem to promise?

See if you can find a modern magazine advertisement for underwear. Are the messages the same? How have the images changed, and how might that affect how people choose their undies?

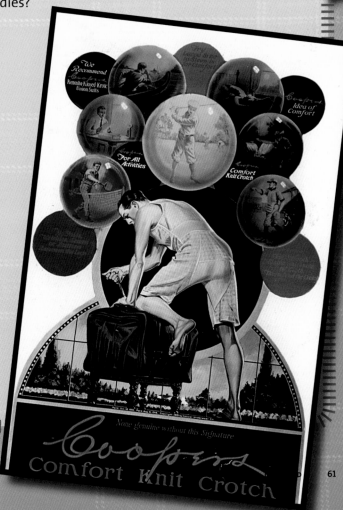

61

Do they make bulletproof ones?

Chapter 5

WARTIME WEAR

As the 1900s began, fashion was changing faster than you could say "knickerbockers." Across Europe and North America, people were reveling in a strong economy, new social freedoms, and amazing technological advances. They were looking for styles that were fun and unique enough for an evolving world. Meanwhile, people in Asia were adopting Western styles of dress, trying to impress their new European and North American trading partners.

Then World War I shook society to its underpants—literally. Women cast off their corsets and bulky clothes so they could work like men on farms and in factory jobs. Men left their union suits behind and went to battle in briefs. Around the world, people were changing to skimpier skivvies.

QUESTION 30

How can we get those curves?

THE 20TH CENTURY HAD ARRIVED. Finally, activists and health officials were convincing women to loosen their corsets. Tiny waists were out. But even if they were letting their natural body shapes show, women still wanted hourglass figures. So, big breasts were in!

Some women tried bust pads made of cotton, celluloid, or rubber to help emphasize their chests. Others used a contraption called a "lemon cup bust improver." From the outside, this looked like a rectangular pouch with a round, padded cup at either end. Inside each cup was a loose spring and horsehair stuffing—just what every girl needed to keep her breasts pointing out. Wearing the device under an evening gown wasn't exactly comfortable, but it did give the impression of a larger bust.

More moderate women could choose between a padded camisole or what was known as a "bust bodice." This was a garment that stretched from the waist up to the underarms, and it was boned and pleated so that it pressed the breasts together to create one smooth curve. Gradually, bust bodices became known as brassieres—the grandmothers of today's bras.

ABREAST OF THE TIMES

1000 CE
A WOMAN IN MONGOLIA DURING THE LING DYNASTY WAS ENTOMBED IN A PADDED BRA, WHICH LOOKED AMAZINGLY SIMILAR TO THE SIMPLE BRAS OF TODAY. MADE OF COTTON AND EMBROIDERED WITH FINE GOLD THREAD, IT SURVIVED TO ASTONISH ARCHAEOLOGISTS A THOUSAND YEARS LATER.

2500 BCE
WOMEN IN ANCIENT CRETE WORE BANDS OF CLOTH DESIGNED TO LIFT AND SUPPORT THEIR BREASTS.

1400
EUROPEAN WOMEN OF FASHION TUCKED STUFFED SILK POUCHES INTO THEIR TOPS SO THEIR BREASTS WOULD LOOK BIGGER.

1863
AMERICAN LUMAN CHAPMAN PATENTED THE FIRST MODERN BREAST SUPPORTER, WHICH HE UNIMAGINATIVELY CALLED THE "CORSET SUBSTITUTE."

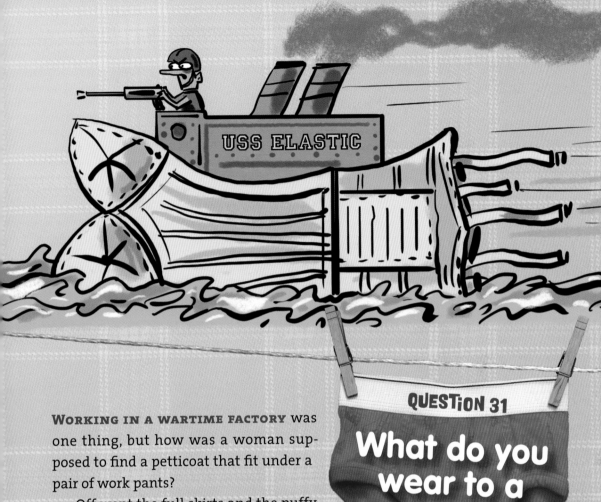

WORKING IN A WARTIME FACTORY was one thing, but how was a woman supposed to find a petticoat that fit under a pair of work pants?

Off went the full skirts and the puffy pantaloons, and on went more utilitarian knickers and drawers. The last of the corsets were tossed away, too. For one thing, these waist-cinchers were using valuable steel for their supports, and that was a wartime waste! In 1917, when the U.S. War Industries Board asked American women to stop buying corsets, it expected to save about 28,000 tonnes (31,000 tons) of metal—enough to build two entire battleships.

The world of women's undergarments was permanently transformed.

QUESTION 31

What do you wear to a war job?

UNDRESS FOR SUCCESS

In the 1920s, Mahatma Gandhi was leading a non-violent but determined movement to throw off British rule and gain independence for India. To help accomplish this, Gandhi encouraged his followers to throw away or burn their British-made clothes. Even though he had lived overseas for many years, Gandhi began wearing traditional Indian loincloths made of handspun cotton.

In 1931, Gandhi met with King George V of England. When a reporter asked if he had felt underdressed wearing only his loincloth and a shawl, Gandhi answered, "The King had on enough for both of us."

QUESTION 32

Who broached the bra idea?

NINETEEN-YEAR-OLD MARY "POLLY" PHELPS JACOB bought a semi-see-through dress to wear to a party in 1913. But there was a problem: her bone-stiffened bodice was showing through. After experimenting for a while, she and her maid tied two silk handkerchiefs together with pink ribbon—and created one of the world's first modern bras. She ditched the bodice and wore her new, almost-backless brassiere to the party.

Over the next year, Polly refined her invention into two loose cups connected by small straps. She patented the idea, launched it on the market, and sold a few hundred bras before selling her design to Connecticut's Warner Brothers Corset Company for $1500.

Polly didn't exactly "invent" the bra. Breast lifters and shapers in various forms already existed around the world. Way back in 1863, an American named Luman Chapman had patented a breast supporter. He didn't mass-produce his new invention, and most women had no idea it existed, but his patent gives him a place in history as the inventor of the first modern bra.

What Polly *did* create was the first bra to sell—and sell well.

QUESTION 33

Can we have some support here, please?

POLLY'S HANDKERCHIEF-TURNED-BRA DESIGN didn't offer much support for women with larger chests. In 1920, New Jersey dress-shop owners Ida Rosenthal and Enid Bissett wanted something better, something that would show off a woman's curves. They created a bra with two shaped cups, connected by elastic. The creation was sewn into the linings of the shop's dresses.

Next, Ida's husband, William, had a look at the design. He suggested adding straps and selling the bra separately. Customers agreed. By 1925, William Rosenthal had patented the world's first seamed "up-lift" bra, the Maidenform Brassiere.

Eventually the bra grew so popular that Ida and Enid gave up their dress shop to focus entirely on underwear manufacturing. Their company still exists today.

DREAMY BRAS

I dreamed I could do anything in my Maidenform bra!

In the 1940s and 1950s, Maidenform ran a series of ads that quickly became famous—ads suggesting that women wearing the company's bras could do just about anything. "I dreamed I was a toreador in my Maidenform bra," read one, featuring a woman swinging her red cape aloft like a bullfighter. "I dreamed I went on safari in my Maidenform bra," read another. Women in this campaign dreamed about winning Academy Awards, performing magic tricks, riding roller coasters, and playing in orchestras. Today the ads offer an interesting glimpse at the progress of feminism and the ambitions of women at the time.

QUESTION 34

How do you lose your shirt?

IN THE EARLY 1900s, men were hot. Literally. While a union suit was cozy in the winter, it was stifling in summer, no matter how light the material or how short the sleeves.

Two things helped change men's underwear around this time. The first was boxing. Boxers were beginning to spring around the ring wearing only loose shorts, and their fans took notice.

Then American soldiers fighting in World War I complained that their union suits were too hot, so the government issued them button-up shorts. By the time they came home, the men were no longer used to wearing one-piece undies—they wanted something lighter and looser.

The new age of underpants had begun.

ⓅⓅ **Private Part**

In the Vietnam War, some American soldiers found the jungle too hot and humid for underwear. Ever since, the phrase "going commando" has meant going without underwear.

100% Cotton

UNDERPANTS iN THE PACiFiC

In World War II, the Japanese army uniform included the *fundoshi*—the same loincloth that had been worn in ancient Japan. Also called a "breechclout," the simple white rectangle of fabric was wrapped between the legs and around the waist with an attached string. For cold weather, Japanese soldiers were also issued long cotton underwear with ties at the waist and ankles.

Does my bum look small in this?

 Private Part

During the 1920s—also known as the "Roaring Twenties"—the new, rebellious "flapper" look called for a slim, boyish figure. Dresses emphasized straight lines, with no lumps or bumps or bell-like skirts. To achieve the fashionable style, many women wore bust flatteners instead of bust enhancers.

100% Cotton

What is a knickerbocker?

SWIMMING. ICE SKATING. SKIING. CYCLING. DANCING. As World War I ended, women embraced all sorts of new opportunities. Health was in style. Exercise was cool. And no self-respecting tennis player could hit a proper serve in a full skirt.

To go with their shorter hemlines and tighter styles—and to stay warm and comfortable on the skating rink—women turned to a new underwear option: knickerbockers. These thigh-length gathered underpants showed more skin than ever before.

At first, knickerbockers looked liked a style worn by English schoolgirls—long, functional, and plain. But as the 1920s brought a new sense of fashion fun to the world, more options hit the store shelves. Women could choose shorter knickers, often made from thin fabric and decorated with flounces and lace. They could copy the ladies of France and wear "camiknickers," which were a lacy combination of camisole and loose undershorts, similar to what we would call "baby-doll" pajamas today. Or, if they wanted to hide a little extra weight, they could choose hip girdles, made from cloth with elastic side panels to help suck in the hips.

QUESTION 36

Why ask Y?

JUST IMAGINE—men's shorts that combined the support of a jock strap with the comfort of union-suit bottoms. When the Cooper Underwear Company introduced Jockey briefs in 1935, the style seemed downright revolutionary. The Y-shaped vent in the front was more secure than the flap used in union suits, but still convenient enough for a quick bathroom break. And this underwear was small. Brief. *Really* brief.

When one of the managers of Chicago's Marshall Field department store arrived at work in the midst of the year's worst blizzard and found Jockey briefs hanging in the store's display windows, he was shocked. They were the skimpiest pairs of men's underwear he had ever seen. Just looking at them made the manager chilly. He demanded that his staff remove the window display immediately. But there was no time—the store was suddenly swamped! Despite the storm, men were crowding through the doors to buy . . . Jockey briefs.

Six hundred packages sold that day. In the next three months, 30,000 pairs disappeared from the store shelves. They were so popular that the company flew shipments to key stores in a private plane it called the *Mascu-liner.* Cooper changed its company name to Jockey, and briefs made their way into the stores of 120 countries around the world.

Welcome to Jockey Air. Please fasten your underwear.

TARGET PRACTICE

When Jockey shorts were sent to soldiers fighting overseas in World War II, the military soon discovered a design flaw—the shorts were white. Flapping above a trench on a roughly rigged clothesline, they made a perfect target for enemy fire. Jockey quickly switched to an olive green fabric and the clotheslines went camouflage.

Private Part

Pop artist Andy Warhol—the one famous for painting Campbell's soup cans—loved Jockey briefs. He even used a pair as a canvas, painting a large dollar sign on it.

100% Cotton

Have you heard the buzz about the latest fashion?

Who's got girdles?

WAIST-WHITTLING WAS BACK. Decades after women chucked their corsets, a designer named Christian Dior helped bring the "wasp waist" look back into fashion. After all, World War II was over, fabric was no longer scarce, and women—in Dior's opinion—were ready for a New Look. To achieve the tiny middles needed to go with broad shoulders and full skirts, women turned back to corsets, or something a bit more modern: girdles.

Made of thick rubber or reinforced elastic and lace, 1950s girdles were a new way to suck in and smooth the hips, tummy, and waist. Most either attached with hook-and-eye fasteners or rolled on, sort of like giant thick rubber gloves for the middle. Some girdles were so taut that the factory workers who made them were exhausted by trying to stretch the rubber to check the sewing stitches. A company called Knickerknick invented a special hydraulic machine just to flatten the garments for quality control.

The girdle quickly became a standard item of underwear. Teenage girls wore them, old ladies wore them—even pregnant women wore girdles to help "support" their pregnancies (a notion that makes modern doctors cringe). One researcher even claimed that women were scientifically less able than men to stand upright, so they required the extra support of a foundation garment.

THE NAME GAME

A century after the corset went out of style, and generations after the girdle lost its stretch, people are still trying to suck in their guts. There are plenty of "body shapers" in stores today—for women and men. Companies don't call these garments girdles or corsets, because people think of those products as old-fashioned and too restrictive. Instead, the new squishers and squeezers for men are called "slimming tank tops," "compression vests," "abdominal binders," and "support briefs." For women, there's shapewear such as Spanx: slimming rib-high, sometimes knee-length bodysuits made of spandex and nylon.

POWERFUL PANTS

If you were designing a superhero, what kind of underpants would you draw? When the creators of Superman published their first comic in 1938, they chose a pair of red undies over a body-hugging blue suit. Why put the underwear overtop of the clothes? Probably it was so Superman didn't look as if he was wearing a tight blue ballet leotard. The comics themselves offered a few other explanations: the cloth was immune to dangerous forces; the woman who raised Superman sewed the clothes from his baby blankets; the undies came straight from planet Krypton.

When writer Dav Pilkey published his first Captain Underpants book in 1995, he didn't bother with the bodysuit underneath. His hero appeared in plain white briefs.

On a blank piece of paper, try creating your own undie-clad hero. Or, create an entire comic strip!

Chapter 6

ROCK AND ROLL AND REVOLUTION

In the 1950s, elasticized thread and new fabrics such as nylon brought us something new: tight underpants. Suddenly women's underwear could do two things at once. It could look pretty *and* suck in extra flab the way a girdle once had. Meanwhile, men discovered that briefs and undershirts weren't their only options. Thanks to rock stars and movie idols, the times—and the tushes—were a-changin'.

Are those your granny's underpants?

AFTER WORLD WAR II, long-legged pantaloons went out the window and smaller *panties* became the hot fashion trend. Soon women could even buy bra-and-panty sets in matching patterns. At the time, these panties were the height of under-fashion. But if we saw them today, we would call them "granny pants." They were still cut high at the waist and low on the legs.

Things changed again in the 1960s, when teens and young adults ruled the world. Because of postwar baby-making, more than half the population of the entire planet was less than 25 years old. And they didn't want to dress like their parents.

In London, a young designer named Mary Quant changed fashion by opening her own boutique and promoting the "miniskirt," a scandalous new fashion that made grandmas gasp and gave school principals heart attacks.

To go with Mary Quant's miniskirt (and the micro-mini, introduced in 1969), fashionable young women needed smaller panties, ones that wouldn't peek out from under their hemlines. Companies began offering underwear cut higher on the legs and lower at the waist, and panties finally began to look the way they do today.

PEACE AND LOVE, BABY

In the 1960s and 1970s, a new generation of hippies and feminists embraced freedom—including freedom from underwear. They believed that bras and girdles were designed to be attractive to men, not useful to women. So why not throw them away and go without?

At one 1968 protest in front of a Miss America pageant, women dumped bras, makeup, and high-heeled shoes into a trash can while news cameras flashed. Somehow the story got around that the protesters had burned their bras instead of just throwing them away. The stereotype of the "bra-burning feminist"—a slur against outspoken women's rights activists—still lives on today.

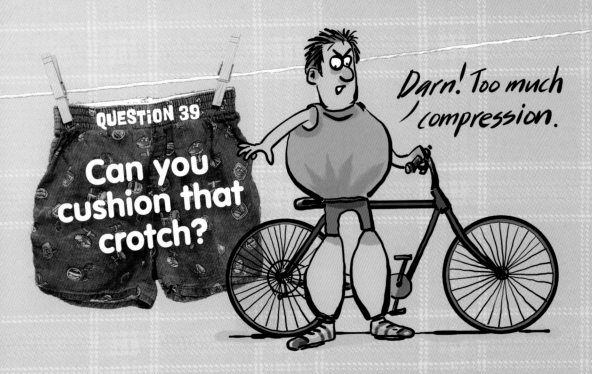

QUESTION 39

Can you cushion that crotch?

Darn! Too much compression.

IN THE 1970s, designers at the Bike Athletic Company (makers of the jock strap) found a new technology in an unusual place—the hospital. Someone noticed that after surgery, doctors wrapped patients' legs in tight, stretchy nylon stockings to prevent blood clots.

Hmmm ... a new stretch fabric? The Bike designers took the stocking material, padded it, and used it for men's underwear, creating what they called "compression shorts." These shorts offered slightly less protection than a jock strap, but the company promised they would help blood circulation, reduce fatigue, and provide support. The shorts were an immediate hit. Casual athletes such as cyclists and softball players adopted the new style. Even the NBA quickly accepted compression shorts as acceptable gear for the basketball court.

Still, many professional athletes kept using the familiar and safer jock strap, or they wore compression shorts over their jocks. By the early 21st century, Bike had sold more than 300 million jock straps around the world.

MORE BOUNCE THAN EVER BEFORE

Sponsored by Lycra

In 1958, a team of scientists at DuPont developed Lycra, a fiber that could be stretched without losing its shape. When pulled, it bounced right back. Lycra (also known as spandex) was intended to replace the rubber in corsets, but corsets were almost extinct by 1958. Instead, the fiber found its niche in swimsuits, ski suits, and, above all, underwear. The new material helped undies fit snugly and snap into place. By the mid-1980s, half of all women's underwear included some Lycra.

Is a ginch a gonch and a gonch a grundie?

THE WAY PEOPLE TALK ABOUT THEIR UNDER-WEAR depends on where they live. In the United States, white briefs are known as "tighty-whities," and a pair of tight bikini briefs might be called a "banana hammock." In western Canada, men and women refer to their skivvies as "gonch" or "gotch." There are a dozen other variations: ginch, gitch, gonchies, gotchies, and gitchies, to name a few. They all seem to have sprung from the Ukrainian word for underwear, which sounds something like *gotchies*.

If you're a North American in Britain, you'll need to be careful when shopping for trousers. If you ask for "pants," you'll end up with underpants. And in England, "vest" means undershirt.

In Australia, undies are named for a millionaire. "Grundies" or "reg grundies" became slang for underpants simply because "undie" rhymes with the name of famous sports commentator and TV producer Reg Grundy. The slang trend began in the 1980s and proved irresistible. Today, there's even an underwear company called Grundies.

Ginch! Gonch! Grundie!

UNDERPANTS AND PRAYERS

Most of us can switch from briefs to boxers or from panties to thongs whenever we want. But what if your underwear is ordained by a higher power?

That's the case for some men and women of the Sikh religion. They believe that there are five main signs of faith. One of these is wearing *kachchhera*, modest cotton underwear held by a drawstring, which is similar for both men and women. Today the pants look much like loose boxer shorts, but some historians suggest that the garment was originally a lot thicker and was worn in gathers to protect sensitive regions from harm while horseback riding or fighting.

In the Mormon religion, initiated believers wear a special suit of underwear known as "temple garments" to protect them from evil. The tradition began with white or beige long-sleeved suits similar to union suits. Today, temple garments usually consist of knee-length drawers and a short-sleeved undershirt. Members of the church are encouraged to wear them as part of their everyday dress.

QUESTION 41
Did someone say "wedgie"?

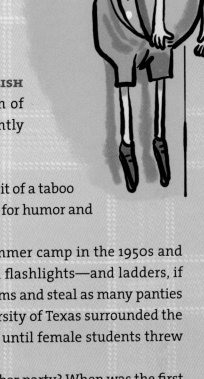

WEDGIE: ACCORDING TO THE OXFORD ENGLISH DICTIONARY, "an act of pulling the cloth of a person's underwear, trousers, etc., tightly between the buttocks..."

Ouch!

Because underwear has always been a bit of a taboo subject, it presents an ongoing opportunity for humor and practical jokes.

Men in college dorms and boys at summer camp in the 1950s and '60s invented the panty raid. Armed with flashlights—and ladders, if necessary—they'd sneak into women's rooms and steal as many panties as possible. In 1961, 2500 men at the University of Texas surrounded the women's dorms and chanted and cheered until female students threw down their underwear.

When was the first bra frozen at a slumber party? When was the first pair of boxer shorts hung from a high school flagpole? No one's been tracking the dates or statistics, but underwear practical jokes are here to stay.

(P/P) **Private Part**

Do you change your underwear on New Year's Eve? In Mexico, you'd put on red underwear if you wanted to find love in the year ahead, and yellow if you wanted to make money. In Venezuela and Ecuador, wearing yellow underwear on New Year's Eve is said to bring good luck.

100% Cotton

QUESTION 42

Do movies make the man?

SOMETIMES ALL IT TAKES is one amazing movie scene to influence the underwear choices of an entire continent. That's what happened with T-shirts in North America. When the U.S. Navy introduced them in the early 1900s, T-shirts were lightweight underwear meant to keep men cool while they were working hard on deck. Regular guys picked up the style in the 1930s, when companies such as Fruit of the Loom sold them to be worn underneath button-down shirts.

Then along came Clark Gable. In 1934, the heart-throb actor took off his shirt on the big screen and revealed his naked chest to the world. Suddenly it was cool to go without an undershirt, and T-shirt sales plummeted!

In the 1950s, blue-jeaned teen rebels Marlon Brando and James Dean appeared in their undershirts with nothing overtop. As men rushed to imitate the movie stars and girls swooned over the simple white shirts, the T went from being underwear to outerwear. And it stayed there.

Movies have changed underwear styles in other countries, too. In the 1990s, India's male "Bollywood" stars danced in everything from G-strings to red boxers, and men's underwear in India hit a whole new level of fashion.

P/P

Private Part

Today, shoppers around the world buy two billion T-shirts a year.

100% Cotton

SCARY SKiVViES

It was him!

In India, the Kachcha Baniyan gang—which translates as the Undershorts-Undershirt gang—has been responsible for murders and robberies in several Indian states. They raid in groups, often in the early morning hours, arming themselves with poles and whatever sticks or clubs they find on the roadside. Their trademark look? They wear only their underwear.

Did boxers arrive in the Nick of time?

IN 1985, NICK KAMEN was a moderately successful British model and a musician. Then he appeared in a TV commercial for Levi's blue jeans. Suddenly Nick was the hunk of the month.

In the ad, Nick stepped into a laundromat and stripped off his jeans to wash them. But it wasn't the jeans that earned Nick fame and fortune—it was his undies.

Levi's had originally intended to put their jeans model in basic white briefs. When the British television censors decided briefs were too . . . well, brief . . . to appear on TV, the Levi's people looked around for a cool alternative. They decided on boxer shorts, a slightly longer and baggier underwear variation invented by a guy named Jacob Golomb in 1925. Jacob had been successful in his business—he founded the company Everlast—but his shorts were popular only with actual ring-fighting boxers. They had never caught on with the public. Until Nick.

When Nick stripped down to show off a pair of sparkling white boxers, sales skyrocketed and every manly man wanted a pair. Then, just a few years later, companies introduced boxer-briefs. This hybrid style gave men the look of boxers—the longer leg and the fashion factor—while offering all the security of a snug pair of briefs.

HIPPIE STYLE

Want to try on some 1970s style? Why not tie-dye a pair of boxer shorts? You'll need an adult to help with the dye for this activity. And be careful—dye can burn.

What you'll need:

- A pair of white boxers
- Rubber bands
- Fabric dye
- Water

What to do:

1. Roll or scrunch up your boxers, securing different parts of the fabric with rubber bands.
2. Prepare the dye according to the directions on the package.
3. Soak the tied-up boxers in dye for about 20 minutes.
4. Without removing the rubber bands, rinse the boxers in tap water until the water runs clear.
5. Carefully remove the rubber bands to reveal your design.

Chapter 7

UNDERWEAR EXPOSÉ

Maybe it all started when
Madonna wore her cone-shaped
bra on stage during a 1980s concert tour, or
when Armani paid soccer star David Beckham millions
of dollars to model his briefs. Somehow, underwear over
the past couple of decades has morphed into something
new. It's a fashion accessory. It's a personality statement.
And it's showing!

Does it make you want to... buy?

In 1982, underwear came out of hiding and onto an enormous billboard in New York City's Times Square. Muscular, larger-than-life men, wearing only tight white briefs, loomed over the traffic. It wasn't the first time Calvin Klein had sparked controversy—the company already had a reputation for using sexually suggestive ads to sell their jeans. And it wouldn't be the last time. In 1992, rapper Marky Mark (in jeans with peeking-out underpants) and model Kate Moss (topless) appeared in a provocative billboard pose. And in 2008, a man clad only in white briefs covered the entire side of a skyscraper on Hong Kong's harbor.

In the world of women's underwear, companies such as Victoria's Secret used similar tactics. In ads and fashion shows, underwear-clad "angels" walked the catwalks in all sorts of revealing lingerie. And it worked! By the 1990s, Victoria's Secret was making more than $1 billion in sales every year.

Both men's and women's brands have worked to link certain styles of underwear with personality types. A man in briefs is conservative. A man in boxer shorts is the free-spirited type. A woman in white panties is innocent, while a woman in a G-string is adventurous. All of this branding is an attempt to entice more customers to buy more underwear, in styles that apparently suit their individual needs.

Even companies that have nothing to do with underwear have used it to sell their products. One Dockers TV ad showed a lineup of men marching in their underwear as they searched for their pants. And in a Bud Light beer ad, men stripped to their skivvies and donated their clothes to charity.

Apparently companies are convinced that we like staring at semi-naked models. But is it true? On the one hand, these ads draw lots of attention. On the other, they've been blamed for causing body-image problems in young people. Studies done by Belgian scientists have found that looking at suggestive underwear and pajama ads damages people's self-esteem.

Meanwhile, we're surrounded by more and more sexually charged underwear advertising. And new stars keep baring their abs in ads—for example, Kellan Lutz of *Twilight* fame stripped to his undies for the 2010 Calvin Klein campaign.

P/P

Private Part

Nudity's not for everyone. In 2007, China banned sexually suggestive ads for women's underwear.

100% Cotton

QUESTION 45

What's under a sari?

THERE ARE 1.4 BILLION PEOPLE in India. If half of them are women, and if many of those women are wearing wrap-around skirts, or saris, there *must* be times when things come accidentally unwrapped!

Traditionally, women in India haven't worn panties. Instead they've donned drawstring underskirts, or petticoats, that look a lot like what North Americans call "peasant skirts." More than one tourist has bought one and mistakenly worn it in public—the equivalent of wearing her underwear on the street. Matched to the color of the sari, the petticoat serves to hold the skirt in place as well as prevent any accidental exposure.

Today many Indian women wear panties as well as petticoats. Some people say this stems from the influence of Christian missionaries. Others say that underwear companies have done such a good job of advertising, they've added a layer to the country's traditional dress. Whatever the cause, a girl in India today is likely wearing one more layer than her great-grandmother did.

Is there a crack in this logic?

A 17-YEAR-OLD BOY was riding his bike down the street in Riviera Beach, Florida. The police pulled him over and handed him a ticket. He had to appear in front of a local judge the next day.

Was he riding dangerously? Had he forgotten his helmet?

No. His pants were too low.

In 2008, Riviera Beach passed a law banning sagging pants that showed more than 10 centimeters (4 inches) of skin or underwear. In other cities with similar laws, the penalties were up to $500 and six months in jail.

Called "saggin'," this way of showing your underwear waistband above low-rise pants probably began in prison, where prisoners aren't allowed to have belts. Hip-hop singers trying to look tough like prisoners adopted the look in the 1990s.

The American Civil Liberties Union protested the new dress laws, claiming that they unfairly targeted African-Americans, since young black males in urban centers were most likely to wear the style. President Obama even chimed in on the issue during an MTV appearance, saying kids should pull up their pants, but also that public officials worrying about saggin' should focus on real problems instead.

At the 2010 Winter Olympics in Vancouver, the Japan Ski Association banned snowboarder Kazuhiro Kokubo from the opening ceremonies— he had altered the official uniform by loosening his tie and lowering his waistband. He basically sagged himself right out of the arena.

oh no! It's a crackdown.

THE UNDERDOG

Kevin Plank opened his first business in high school, selling trinkets at Grateful Dead concerts. Then, as a business student at the University of Maryland, he got tired of working out in a sweat-soaked T-shirt. A year later, in 1996, he launched Under Armour, hoping to use technology to create briefs, undershirts, and T-shirts specifically suited to the needs of athletes. With some key professional football players wearing his gear, Kevin watched his relatively low-budget company blast ahead of Reebok and Nike in the world of performance sports gear. Under Armour is now sold in 14,000 stores around the world.

Gee, what's that?

NO THONG ZONE

THONGS AND G-STRINGS ARE NOTHING NEW. They've been around since women wore cache-sexes in ancient Europe. Historians believe that, back then, these tiny coverings were partly meant to tell men that a woman was mature and available.

It's not so different today!

Strippers and exotic dancers began wearing G-strings in the early 1900s, when the term was pretty much synonymous with "loincloth." In modern usage, a thong and a G-string are almost the same thing, although a thong may be slightly thicker at the back.

The word "thong," originally meaning a strip of cloth or leather, was first used to describe skimpy swimsuits in the 1970s, when women started wearing thong bikinis on the beaches of Brazil (a style the locals called "dental floss"). Gradually the trend spread, though more in the world of underwear than swimwear. For buyers in North America, Asia, and Europe, thongs were seen as fashionable, sexy—and a way to avoid visible panty lines.

Not everyone likes thongs, though. In fact, some high schools have even tried to ban them. In 2002, an assistant principal at a San Diego high school was demoted after she did individual "panty checks" on girls entering a school dance, just to make sure they weren't wearing thongs. Those with inappropriate underwear were sent home to change.

Private Part

A woman whose G-string is showing above the back of her low-rise pants is said to be "T-barring" or showing a "whale's tail."

100% Cotton

UPLiFTiNG DEVELOPMENTS

In 2006, Australia's aussieBum brand released its Wonderjock underwear. Using a play on the Wonderbra name, these briefs were designed to make a man's crotch look larger.

Today, a number of companies cater to men looking for leaner waists, padded behinds, or enhanced crotches. These cushions and paddings may not be as large as King Henry VIII's codpieces, back in the 1500s, but they're still . . . noticeable.

I'd like a free pair, please..

Is there an economics of underwear?

AFTER THE STOCK MARKET crashed in 1929 and the Great Depression began, there was no money to spare—not for extra underwear, anyway. Desperate to tempt new customers, stores began advertising durability and good value. The Marshall Field department store touted a No-Rip brand, with the slogan "No more mending." If your underwear tore, you'd get a free pair.

Today, experts still look to underwear sales as an indicator of economic trends. According to U.S. economics guru Alan Greenspan, when times are tough, men don't buy new underwear. But when brief and boxer sales start to recover, then the economy starts looking better, too!

Apparently that theory doesn't work for women's underwear. The (mostly male) economists theorize that a woman might consider a new pair of panties the perfect inexpensive purchase to make her feel better when money troubles strike.

GETTING THE RUNS

Hawaii underpants Run

Each year in Kona, Hawaii, hundreds of runners show up downtown in only their undies to participate in the Ironman Hawaii Underpants Run. The money raised goes to charity.

 Private Part

In 1985, Joe Boxer printed a thousand pairs of underwear with a pattern of $100 bills—something that broke America's forgery laws. The Secret Service confiscated the boxers before anyone could go shopping with their underwear.

100% Cotton

Where do we go from here?

UNDERWEAR THAT TRACKS YOUR BLOOD PRESSURE. Underwear with a strap for your MP3 player. Armor-like underwear made from soda cans, rivets, and metal clamps. There are so many styles on the market, you could probably wear a new pair of outlandish undies every day for the rest of your life.

Some of the world's newest skivvies are designed for better health. (That's right, we're still following the lead of those all-wool union suits.) Researchers in Britain are working on a bra that can detect tiny temperature changes within the breast, which might indicate the early stages of breast cancer. And according to company claims, the tiny synthetic strands in Japan's nano-fiber underwear can burn away fat through friction. With all of these options, it's surprising that anyone's wearing plain old briefs and panties anymore. Excuse me, but is that your underwear ringing? Oh … you must be wearing one of those new pairs with a cellphone pocket.

UNDIE 500

TAKE YOUR UNDIES TO THE EDGE

A Canadian company called Ginch Gonch sells panties decorated with a design of bacon strips. A Chinese company has found a market for briefs with a zippered pouch in the front, to keep money safe from thieves.

If you could design your own undies, what would they look like? Would they be retro or ultra-modern? Would they be functional or just for fun? Once you've sketched your ideas, try creating a brand name and drawing a magazine ad. Would your skivvies be top sellers?

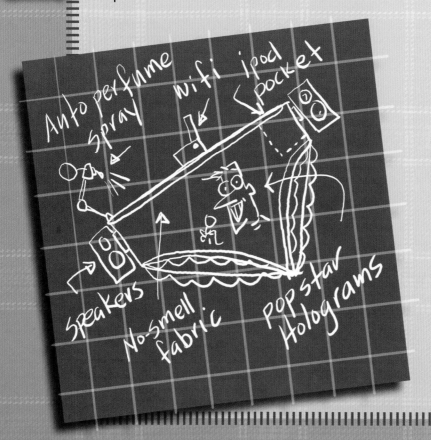

ALL WRAPPED UP

FOR CENTURIES, new underwear styles have appeared whenever social changes sweep the world. Just think—men's briefs were adopted by soldiers during one of history's biggest wars. And women switched their petticoats for bloomers once they left their kitchens and started working in factories or cycling to the tennis courts. So if our underwear reflects our values, our work, and our interests, what's next?

Do spacesuits have skivvies?

IN THE 1960s, when the first astronauts blasted into orbit, they found themselves wriggling in their seats—and not just from excitement. Without gravity, their underwear was riding up. The sleeves of their undershirts crept up their arms while the bottoms of their boxers slid up their thighs.

Jockey stepped in and helped solve the problem with elastic hems at the wrists and thighs. Since then, space-age skivvies have grown more and more sophisticated. Today when astronauts leave their shuttle or space station to work outside—clinging to the metal hull with super-strong magnets—they wear special protective spacesuits. Underneath they wear one-piece long underwear, like the old-fashioned union suit gone cyber. All through the fabric run small tubes filled with water. While astronauts are spacewalking, they encounter the sun's heat without the protection of Earth's atmosphere. The solution? Water is pumped in and out of their underwear tubes to keep them cool.

There are still some undie issues. Shuttles and space stations don't come with washers and dryers, and if you're assigned to a space station for six months, there's no room for you to pack 150 clean pairs. Here's what real astronauts do:

- Wear it again. Most of them change their shorts only once every three to four days. (They claim they don't get as dirty in space.)

- Wash it in a plastic bag. Some astronauts fill a plastic bag with water, add undies and soap, and shake, shake, shake until the dirt comes out.

Private Part

NASA scientists are working to find bacteria that will eat cotton. Then, when astronauts' underwear gets dirty, they can feed it to the bugs.

100% Cotton

LUNAR LAUNDRY

What if your underwear gets dirty in space and you don't feel like hand-washing? You might throw it in the cosmic garbage. Stuff it into a small rocket with the rest of the space station debris, then blast the rocket into Earth's atmosphere, where it burns to bits. Some space-goers get creative. One wrapped his undies in paper, dribbled some water on them, and planted seeds inside. They sprouted in just a couple of days.

Further Reading

Daynes, Katie. *The Revealing Story of Underwear*. London: Usborne
  Publishing, 2006.

Joe Boxer. *A Brief History of Shorts*. San Francisco: Chronicle Books, 1995.

Shaskan, Kathy. *How Underwear Got Under There*. New York: Dutton
  Children's Books, 2007.

Swain, Ruth Freeman. *Underwear*. New York: Holiday House, 2008.

Whitty, Helen. *Underwear*. South Yarra: MacMillan Education Australia,
  2000.

Bibliography

Arak, Joel. "Panty-Check Principal Demoted." CBS News website. www.cbsnews.com/stories/2002/06/18/national/main512654.shtml (accessed August 11, 2010).

Ashenburg, Katherine. *The Dirt on Clean*. Toronto: Alfred A. Knopf Canada, 2007.

Carter, Alison. *Underwear*. New York: Drama Book Publishers, 1992.

Chenoune, Farid. *Hidden Underneath*. New York: Assouline Publishing, 2005.

Cremers–Van der Does, Eline Canter. *The Agony of Fashion*. Poole: Blandford Press, 1980.

Dens, Nathalie, Patrick Pelsmacker, and Wim Janssens. "Effects of Scarcely Dressed Models in Advertising on Body Esteem for Belgian Men and Women." *Sex Roles*, March 2009, pp. 366–378.

Dingus, Anne. "Mentionables." *Texas Monthly*, November 2004, pp. 88–94.

Elliot, Lynne. *Clothing in the Middle Ages*. New York: Crabtree Publishing, 2004.

Ewing, Elizabeth. *Underwear*. New York: Theatre Arts Books, 1972.

Farrell, Jeremy. *Socks and Stockings*. London: B. T. Batsford, 1992.

Farrell-Beck, Jane, and Colleen Gau. *Uplift*. Philadelphia: University of Pennsylvania Press, 2002.

Fischer, Gayle V. *Pantaloons and Power*. Kent, Ohio: Kent State University Press, 2001.

Grass, Milton N. *History of Hosiery*. New York: Fairchild Publications, 1955.

Harris, Chris. "Barack Obama Weighs in on Sagging-Pants Ordinances." MTV website. www.mtv.com/news/articles/1598462/20081103/story.jhtml (accessed August 11, 2010).

Hawthorne, Rosemary. *Knickers*. London: Souvenir Press, 1985.

Hermkens, Anna-Karina. "Gendered Objects." *Journal of Pacific History*, June 2007, pp.1–20.

Hewitt, Mike. *Uniforms and Equipment of the Imperial Japanese Army in World War II*. Atglen, Pennsylvania: Schiffer Publishing, 2002.

Horovitz, Bruce. "Super Bowl Ad Stars Leave Pants on the Ground." *USA Today*, January 27, 2010, p. 3.

Hounshell, David A., and John Kenly Smith, Jr. "The Nylon Drama." *Invention and Technology*, Fall 1998, pp. 40–55.

"India: Kacha Banian (Kucha Banyan) or Underwear-Undershirt Wearing Group or Shorts-Underwear Clad Group." Immigration and Refugee Board of Canada website. www.unhcr.org/refworld/docid/3df4be4118.html (accessed August 5, 2010).

Johnston, Lucy. "The Secret History of the Corset and Crinoline." Victoria and Albert Museum website. www.fathom.com/course/21701726/index.html.

Kippen, Cameron. "The History of Footwear: Hosiery." Curtin University of Technology website. www.podiatry.curtin.edu.au/tight.html#eve.

Lester, Katherine, and Bess Viola Oerke. *Accessories of Dress*. New York: Dover Publications, 2004.

Lord, William Berry. *Freaks of Fashion*. Mendocino, California: R. L. Shep, 1993.

"No Washers or Dryers in Space." NASA website. www.nasa.gov/audience/forkids/home/F_No_Washers_Dryers_in_Space.html#bctop.

Pendergast, Sara, and Tom Pendergast, eds. *Fashion, Costume, and Culture*. Detroit: UXL, 2004.

"Polish Museum Unveils Exhibit on . . . Underwear." Fox News website. www.foxnews.com/story/0,2933,332828,00.html (accessed August 3, 2010).

Sharma, Kabeer. "A Brief History." *Open Magazine*, October 10, 2009.

Smith, Virginia. *Clean*. Oxford: Oxford University Press, 2007.

Steele, Valerie, ed. *Encyclopedia of Clothing and Fashion*. Detroit: Charles Scribner's Sons, 2005.

Vara, John. "In Praise of Wool Underwear." *Yankee*, January/February 2001, p. 96.

Velden, Patrik Vander. "Horace Greeley Johnson: 'Edison of Underwear.'" Vintage Skivvies website. www.vintageskivvies.com/pages/archives/articles/newsstoriesfromyesteryear/edisonofunderwear.html.

Willett, C., and Phillis Cunnington. *The History of Underclothes*. London: Faber and Faber, 1951.

Index

Adam and Eve 16
advertising 60, 61, 69, 91, 92–93, 94
Africa 9
  see also Namibia; Nigeria
al-Din Shah, Nasir, King of Persia 31
Araweté people 10
armor 23, 25
Asia 24, 32, 62, 97
  see also China; India; Japan
astronauts 104–105
attigi 54
aussieBum 98

baleen see whalebone
bamboo 24
bathing 18–19, 24, 55
Beckham, David 91
Belgium 22
Bennett, C. F. 58
Bike Athletic Company 81
Bike Web Company 58
Bissett, Enid 68
Bloomer, Amelia 46–47, 48
bloomers 3, 46–47, 48, 49, 103
body image 93
body odor 18–19, 20, 22
body shapers 76
boxer-briefs 88, 89

boxer shorts 2, 70, 85, 86, 88, 89, 90, 93, 99
Brando, Marlon 86
bras 3, 8, 63, 64, 67, 68, 80, 85
  bra burning 80
  see also brassieres; bust bodices; lemon cup bust improver
brassieres 63
Brazil 10
breechclout
  see fundoshi
breeches 2, 12, 18
briefs 2, 62, 73, 74, 88, 89, 91, 92–93, 99, 103
  Jockey briefs 73, 89
  Y-front 2, 73
brocade 32, 39
Brummell, Beau 36
bum rolls 33
burlap 51
busks 34
bust bodices 63
bust flatteners 71
bustles 31, 43
buttons 57
cache-sexe 8, 97
calf pads 29
Calvin Klein 92
camiknickers 72
camisoles 63
Canada 54, 83, 102
Capone, Al 89

Captain Underpants 77
celluloid 63
chain mail 23
Chapman, Luman 64, 67
chemise 34, 35
China 6, 24–25, 64, 93, 102
codpieces 30
compression shorts 81
Cooper Underwear Company 56, 73
Coopers Union Suits 61
corsets 3, 28, 34–35, 37, 45, 62, 63, 65, 75, 76
  for men 36, 76
cotton 24, 54, 63, 66
Crete 35, 64
crinolines 3, 40, 43, 45
  cage crinoline 40–41, 42, 43, 44

dandies 36
da Volterra, Daniele 17
de Joinville, Jean 20
de' Medici, Catherine 34–35
Dean, James 86
Denmark 8
Dior, Christian 75
doublets 29, 30
drawers 41, 49, 65
Dunlop Rubber Company 57
DuPont 82

economics 99
Egypt 4, 6, 7, 10
elastic 57, 75, 104
  elasticized thread 78
England 41, 43, 48, 49
  see also Henry VIII;
    Victoria, Queen of
    England
Etruscan civilization 10
Europe 5, 15, 18–19, 25, 26,
  31, 32, 38, 43, 45, 62, 64,
  97
  see also Belgium;
    England; France;
    Germany; Italy;
    Rome
Everlast 88

fabrics 24, 25, 32, 33, 51,
  52–53, 54, 78
  see also brocade;
    burlap; cotton; hemp;
    linen; Lycra; nylon;
    silk; spandex; taffeta;
    wool
farthingales 32, 35, 37,
  40–41
fig leaves 16–17
fleas 18, 24
France 8, 19, 20, 34–35, 72
freedom dress 47
Fruit of the Loom 60, 86
fundoshi 6, 71

Gable, Clark 86
gambesons 23, 29
Gandhi, Mahatma 66
garters 2, 57
George V, King of
  England 66
Germany 37
  see also Henry IV
Ginch Gonch 102
girdles 3, 75, 76, 80
  hip girdles 72
gladiators 11, 14
Golomb, Jacob 88
Goodyear, Charles 57
Gregory VII, Pope 21
Grundies 83
Grundy, Reg 83
G-strings 86, 93, 97
Hancock, Thomas 57
Hawaii Underpants Run
  100
Heidelberg Electric Belt
  59
hemp 19
Henry II, King of France
  34
Henry IV, King of
  Germany 21
Henry VIII, King of
  England 29, 30, 98

Inca civilization 6
India 37, 66, 86, 87, 94
Inuit peoples 54
Isabella, Princess of
  Spain 22
Italy 10

Jacob, Mary Phelps 67
Jaeger, Dr. Gustav 52–53
Japan 6, 24, 25, 39, 71, 101
  fundoshi 6, 71
  mawashi 7
jill straps 59
jock straps 58, 59, 73, 81
Jockey 73, 74, 89, 104
Joe Boxer 100
Johnson, Horace Greeley
  56

Kachcha Baniyan gang
  87
kachchhera 84
Kamen, Nick 88
Kenosha Klosed Krotch
  56
  see also union suits
Khan, Genghis 25
kimonos 24, 39
knickerbockers 62, 72
  see also bloomers;
    pantaloons
Knickerknick 75
knickers 57, 65, 72
  see also drawers;
    panties
knights 12, 23
Kokubo, Kazuhiro 95

laundry 18–19, 21, 22, 39, 57, 74
in space 105
lemon cup bust improver 63
lice 18
linen 18–19
loincloths 2, 5, 6, 9, 10–11, 12, 15, 26, 66, 97
fundoshi 6, 71
materials 6, 8
mawashi 7
subligaculum 10–11, 14
see also cache-sexe, maro
long johns 50, 53
Louis XIV, King of France 19
Lutz, Kellan 93
Lycra 82

Madonna 91
Maidenform 68–69
Mali 8
Marky Mark 92
maro 9
mawashi 7
Mayan civilization 6
Mediterranean 10
Michelangelo 16–17
Middle Ages 18–19, 20–21
Middle East 32
see also Persia
Miller, Elizabeth Smith 46–47
missionaries 26

Moss, Kate 92
mummies 4, 5

nagajuban 39
Namibia 26
nanofiber 101
Nigeria 26
North America 6, 26, 41, 43, 45, 50, 55, 62, 86, 97
see also Canada; United States
nudity, attitudes toward 15, 16–17
nylon 76, 78

panniers 37, 38
pantaloons 46–47, 65, 79
see also bloomers
panties 2, 79, 85, 93, 94, 99
granny pants 79
panty raids 85
thongs 3, 97
see also drawers
pants 13
Papua New Guinea 9
Pearl, Mr. 36
Persia 13, 31
petticoats 3, 18, 32, 37, 38, 39, 40, 45, 48, 65, 94, 103
Pilkey, Dav 77
Plank, Kevin 96
plate mail 23
Polynesia 9, 26
Pope Gregory VII 21

Quant, Mary 79
qulittaq 54

ramie 24
Rational Dress Society 49
Renaissance 16–17
Rome 8, 10–11, 12, 13
Rosenthal, Ida and William 68
royalty 33
see also Catherine de' Medici; George V; Henry II; Henry IV; Henry VIII; Isabella; Louis XIV; Nasir al-Din Shah; Victoria
rubber 57, 63, 75

saggin' 95
satin 32
sewing, history of 5, 8
shifts 18
silk 25, 32, 39
South America 9, 10
see also Brazil
spandex 76
Spanx 76
Stanton, Elizabeth Cady 46–47
subligaculum 10–11
Sullivan, John L. 50, 51
Superman 77
suspenders 2

Tahiti 26
temple garments 84
Teuton civilization 12
Thompson, W. S. 40
thongs 3, 97, 98
   see also G-strings
tights 2, 29, 30
tie-dye 90
Tomalin, Lewis 52–53, 54,
   60
T-shirts 86, 96
tunics 12, 23
Turkey 25
Tutankhamen 7

Under Armour 96
undershirts 21, 29, 33, 35,
   49, 53
   see also chemise;
     gambesons; shifts;
     T-shirts
union suits 2, 53, 54, 55, 56,
   57, 60, 70, 101
   wool 2, 52–53, 101
United States 83

velvet 32
Venus of Lespugue 8
Victoria, Queen of
   England 43, 48
Victoria's Secret 92
Vietnam War 70

waistbands 10
   see also cache-sexe,
     maro
Warhol, Andy 74
Warner Brothers Corset
   Company 67
wedgie 85
whalebone 34, 35
Wonderjock 98
wool 2, 52–53
World War I 62, 65, 70, 72
World War II 71, 74, 75, 79

About the Author

TANYA LLOYD KYI prefers polka dots over plaid, solid over striped, and cotton over polyester. She has been known to work in her pyjamas, but not in only her underwear—it would be much too chilly. She once appeared in front of a large crowd wearing only her skivvies and everyone pointed and laughed . . . Wait. That was a bad dream.

Properly dressed or not, she has managed to write more than a dozen books for children and teens. Her interests include science and social issues and her previous publications include *50 Burning Questions, 50 Poisonous Questions,* and *True Stories from the Edge: Fires!*

Tanya is an accomplished baker, a terrible singer, and a slowly improving gardener. She lives in Vancouver, B.C., with her husband, Min, and their two children.

About the Illustrator

ROSS KINNAIRD has illustrated over twenty-five books for children. When asked how he comes up with his ideas, he replies that he sits in a bath of warm lemonade with a frozen chicken on his head!

The thing he enjoys most about being an illustrator is visiting schools to talk about books and drawing funny pictures of teachers. He has been to about 150 schools and spoken to thousands of kids.

He loves to travel and has visited Australia, Israel, Morocco, and countries throughout Asia and Europe.

If you like asking questions, check out these other books in the 50 Questions series:

50 BURNING QUESTIONS:
A SIZZLING HISTORY OF FIRE

by Tanya Lloyd Kyi

Illustrated by Ross Kinnaird

"(A) lighthearted, informative look at a fascinating subject ... Accessibly written and appealingly designed ..."
—*Kirkus Reviews*

"A fun and informative book for anyone fascinated by fire, which means pretty much everyone."
—*Booklist*

How do you squeeze fire from a stone?
By striking a piece of flint against a rock to create a spark.

Why did firefighters need beards?
So they could pull the hair over their mouths and filter air when they were in thick smoke.

If you're burning with curiosity to find out what kind of salt explodes, how to send your breath through a glass jar, or whether people really can walk on coals, check out *50 Burning Questions*, brimming with hilarious cartoons, cool activities, and red-hot information.

Paperback $12.95 | Hardcover $21.95

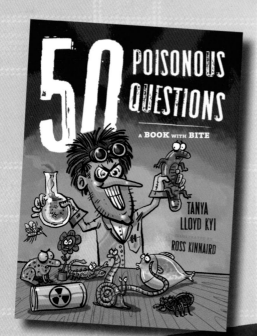

50 POISONOUS QUESTIONS:
A BOOK WITH BITE

by Tanya Lloyd Kyi

Illustrated by Ross Kinnaird

"As previously demonstrated by last year's fun-filled *50 Burning Questions: A Sizzling History of Fire*, Tanya Lloyd Kyi has no trouble balancing the sinister and the safe."
—*Quill & Quire*

Should you pee on a jellyfish sting?

Even though some people think so, it's not true. Douse it with vinegar.

Can Gila monsters cure diabetes?

Yes, a drug used to treat the disease comes from the Gila monster's venom.

The good news is that in the entire world, there is not a single venomous creature intentionally hunting humans.

Come step into the world of lethal leaves and murderous minerals, where you will discover intriguing facts, killer cartoons, and poisonous puzzles. But be warned!

Do not kiss golden dart frogs.

Paperback $12.95 | Hardcover $21.95